WORD GAMES

ALSO BY GYLES BRANDRETH

Classic Puzzles
The Book of Solo Games

WORD GAMES

Gyles Brandreth

PERENNIAL LIBRARY

Harper & Row, Publishers, New York
Cambridge, Philadelphia, San Francisco, Washington
London, Mexico City, São Paulo, Singapore, Sydney

LIBRARY OF CONGRESS CATALOG CARD NUMBER: 86-46047
ISBN: 0-06-055069-4   87 88 89 90 91 MPC 10 9 8 7 6 5 4 3 2 1
ISBN: 0-06-096176-7 (PBK.)   87 88 89 90 91 MPC 10 9 8 7 6 5 4 3 2 1

For John Meade

CONTENTS

PART TWO: WRITTEN GAMES 41

PART THREE: WORD PLAY 93

Foreword

Of the world's five thousand languages, English may not be the most widely used – 695 million people speak Northern Chinese! – but it is the richest by far. The English language contains some 500,000 different words, plus a further 300,000 or so technical terms. By contrast, the Germans have a vocabulary of just 185,000 words and the poor French struggle along with under 100,000 – and that's including such gems of *franglais* as *les blugines, le weekend* and *le camping*.

However, while there are over 400 million people who speak English on the planet, very few of them seem to be taking full advantage of the wonderfully rich language that lies at their disposal. Shakespeare managed to use over 30,000 different words in his plays and James Joyce used over 30,000 in *Ulysses* alone, but a recent statistical study of telephone speech among contemporary Americans revealed that a vocabulary of only 737 words was used in 96 per cent of all conversation. At full stretch, the average educated Briton, American or Australian is unlikely to use more than 5,000 words in speech and 10,000 in written communications.

It was because I was wanting to increase my own vocabulary (and that of my children), and because, too, I wanted to exploit a little more fully the wonderfully rich potential of our language, that I began to compile this book. I have found that playing with words helps me to understand them better and enjoy them more. The first two sections contain specific word games – all the classic games and old family favourites you would expect to find, plus, I hope, a number of interesting surprises – while the final section features 'word play', ways of enjoying words that cannot strictly be classified as games but are, I trust, entertaining and stimulating nonetheless. The idea is that you should use the material in this section as the springboard for devising your own word games and forms of word play.

I believe we would value our language more if we enjoyed it more, and that's really all the book is about: encouraging people to have fun with words. Language, after all, is one of the very few things that distinguishes us from the rest of the animal kingdom, so it seems a shame not to take full advantage of it. As Bertrand Russell sagely observed, 'However eloquently a dog may bark, he cannot tell you that his parents were poor but honest.'

G.B.

PART ONE
SPOKEN GAMES

Party Games

I Love My Love

In the traditional version of this game the players take it in turn to describe their loved one using different letters of the alphabet, like this:

GEORGE: I love my love with an A because she is Arabella from Austria and amazingly ambitious.

BERNARD: I love my love with a B because she is Bernadette from Birmingham and bountifully buxom.

SHAW: I love my love with a C because she is Chloe from California and completely crazy.

In the wordsmith's version of the game the players continue with the same letter of the alphabet until they have exhausted it. Starting at A they take it in turn to think of adjectives beginning with A to describe their loved one and go on and on until one of them cannot think of a fresh adjective beginning with A or repeats an adjective already used. He loses a point and all the players move on to the next letter. When the players have reached the letter Z, or have stopped play after eight hours having only reached C, the player who has lost least points becomes the winner.

For those with rich vocabularies (and for those seeking to acquire them) this is a very entertaining game, as you can see from the first moments of this contest:

GEORGE: I love my love with an A because she is Abandoned!

BERNARD: – Able!

SHAW: – Amiable!

GEORGE: – Artful!

BERNARD: – Accommodating!

SHAW: – Acceptable!

GEORGE: – Adaptable!

BERNARD: – Accomplished!

SHAW: – Adulterous!

GEORGE: – Affluent!

BERNARD: – Advanced!

SHAW: – Amorous!

GEORGE: – Affable!

BERNARD: – Aristocratic!

SHAW: – Aromatic!

GEORGE: – Autonomous!

BERNARD: – Autocratic!

SHAW: – Available!

GEORGE: – Appealing!

BERNARD: – Astonishing!

SHAW: – Artful!

GEORGE: – Angelic!

BERNARD: – Altruistic!

SHAW: – Asleep!

GEORGE: – Ascetic!

BERNARD: – Aesthetic!

SHAW: – Amorous!

By making his love 'amorous' Shaw has repeated one of the attributes already ascribed to her, so the time has come to move on to B and we shall never know whether the young lady was also assured, attainable, awesome, audible, attenuated, artificial, acute, animated, acquiescent or abstinent.

Backwards Spelling

At the best of times, spelling words like Parallel, Separate, Embarrassed, Desiccate and Sacrilegious presents all but a few of us with problems. Spelling the words *backwards* would seem to be asking altogether too much – but that's just what this amusing party game is all about.

The players take it in turn to be given a word and have to spell it backwards. They must start to speak as soon as they have been told the word and they must not hesitate or correct themselves while they are speaking. Every time a player spells a word backwards correctly he scores a point. After ten rounds, the player with the highest score is the winner.

Inexperienced players will find even the simplest six- and seven-letter words a challenge and everyone will find words like these nearly impossible:

Abbreviation	Nonconformity
Blunderbuss	Onomatopoiea
Dilatory	Quintessential
Evangelistic	Rumbustious
Fluorescence	Subpoena
Graphology	Tautological
Hypocrisy	Unintentional
Ingratiating	Vaporousness
Juvenescence	Whomsoever
Kaleidoscope	Yarborough
Laryngitis	Zincograph

An umpire should be appointed before the game begins to select the words to be spelt and to make sure that they are being spelt backwards in the correct order.

The Last Shall Be First

The players decide on a category – Countries, Animals, Flowers, Scientists, Amino-acids or whatever. The first player calls out a word belonging in the chosen category, followed by each of the other players in turn. The catch is that the first letter of each word must be the same as the final letter of the preceding word. No word may be repeated. A player is out if he cannot think of a suitable word, if he repeats a word, or if he calls out a word that does not fit the category.

For example, with three players, and with Countries as the category, a game might begin like this:

DAVID:	Germany
HERBERT:	Yugoslavia
LAWRENCE:	Australia
DAVID:	Aden
HERBERT:	Nepal
LAWRENCE:	Luxembourg
DAVID:	Greece
HERBERT:	Egypt

Adverbs

One player leaves the room while the others agree among themselves on a suitable adverb. The player who has left the room then comes in again and has to guess the chosen word. To get some clues he or she may ask each of the other players in turn three questions (about any subject at all) to which the other player must reply in the manner suggested by the chosen adverb.

When each player has been asked three questions and all have replied in the appropriate manner, the outsider has to guess the adverb. As a refinement, he may be allowed three guesses, scoring three points if he gets the word right first time, two points if his second guess is correct, and one point if he guesses correctly at his last attempt. The other players then take it in turn to leave the room while another adverb is chosen.

The adverbs chosen should be descriptive and not too obscure, because everyone likes to guess words if they possibly can, and it's a good idea to let everyone have a go.

If you are stuck for ideas, here are some suggested adverbs, which might also suggest other suitable words to you:

angrily	hesitantly	proudly
childishly	humbly	rudely
conspiratorially	lazily	seductively
emotionally	lovingly	stridently
furtively	poetically	thoughtfully
gaily	pompously	timidly

Tennis, Elbow, Foot

The players take it in turn to call out a word which is either directly associated with the word previously called out or which rhymes with it. For example: Tennis, Elbow, Foot, Ball, Game, Bird, Third, Man, Handle, Candle, Light, Weight, etc.

Players are out if they hesitate, if they call out a word that neither relates to the previous word nor rhymes with it, or if they repeat a word that has previously been called out. A referee may be needed to settle any disputes. The last one left in is the winner.

Fizz-Buzz

FIZZ-BUZZ is a very silly game that is suitable for players of any age. The players take it in turns to call out numbers in ascending order, starting from 1, but replacing every multiple of 3 with the word 'Fizz', every multiple of 5 with the word 'Buzz', and every multiple of the two with the word 'Fizz-Buzz'.

So the sequence goes: One, Two, Fizz, Four, Buzz, Fizz, Seven . . . Fourteen, Fizz-Buzz, Sixteen . . . and so on.

A player is out if he calls a number instead of fizzing or buzzing (or vice versa) or if he confuses his fizzes with his buzzes. The last player left in the game is the winner.

Word Chain

Here is a game for two or more in which the players take it in turn to think of a two-word or three-word phrase, the first word of which must rhyme with the last word of the previous player's phrase. The opening player's first phrase is always 'Word Chain'.

To give you an idea of the game in action, here is a brief two-handed bout between Jack and Jill:

JACK:	˙ Word Chain
JILL:	Grain of wheat
JACK:	Heat wave
JILL:	Slave trade
JACK:	Laid back
JILL:	Sack of coal
JACK:	Pole vault
JILL:	Malt whisky

At this point, Jack gives up because he cannot think of a phrase beginning with a rhyme for 'whisky'. Jill has won the round, and it is her turn to start the next round, again with the opening phrase 'Word chain'.

What constitutes an acceptable phrase and a legitimate rhyme must be left to the commonsense or whim of the individual players.

Word Chain may also be played as a solo game and, when played thus, is a perfect cure for insomnia.

Group Limericks

The first player makes up the opening line of a limerick; the second player has thirty seconds to come up with the next line; the third player another thirty seconds for the third, and so on until the limerick is complete. The verse does not need to make much sense, but it must rhyme and it should scan.

Here's an example of a group limerick created by five passengers flying from London to Madrid, shortly after they had been told the flight was being diverted to Paris. It took them just thirty-five seconds to come up with this:

> There was a young man on a plane
> Who wanted to travel to Spain,
> But they led him a dance
> And took him to France –
> Next time he'll travel by train!

The Moulting Ostrich

A leader is chosen and all he has to do is make the other players smile or laugh. Grinning himself, he says to each player in turn, 'Alas, alas, my poor ostrich is moulting and I don't know what to do.' To this each player must make a reasonable suggestion, keeping a totally straight face all the while. Anyone caught smiling, smirking, giggling or bursting into wild hysterics is disqualified.

When he goes round the second time the leader says, 'Alas, alas, my poor ostrich is moulting and I've got a boil on the end of my nose.' Again each player must make, poker-faced, a reasonable helpful suggestion. For the third round the leader says, 'Alas, alas, my poor ostrich is moulting, I've got a boil on the end of my nose and my turkey's lost its stuffing.' Any player surviving all three rounds is a winner.

Word Order

The first player calls out a word at random, the second player follows with another word suggested by the first word, the third player with another suggested by the second, and so on around the group. If the first word were *apple*, it might be followed by *pie*, *sky*, *blue*, *colour*, *television*, *set*, *match*, *stick*, *cane*, *sugar*, and so on.

After a few rounds the first player suddenly shouts 'Reverse order!' at which point the last player to speak must remember the word before his and all the words are repeated around the groups in reverse order – from *sugar* to *cane* to *stick* to *match* to *set* to *television* to *colour* to *blue* to *sky* to *pie* to *apple*.

Anyone hesitating, getting the words in the wrong order, or forgetting a word loses a life. The player who has lost the fewest lives after five rounds is the winner.

Follow On

The first player calls out a two-word phrase or a word consisting of two separate parts. For example:

White Elephant	Skin Deep
Hard Times	Butterfly
Suitcase	Footpath
Pink Gin	High Tide
Foodstuff	Waterfall

Then each player in turn has to call out another word or phrase starting with the second part of the previous one. If a player cannot think of a suitable word or phrase he may throw out a challenge to the rest of the players. If anyone *does* provide a suitable word or phrase, the player whose turn it was drops out. Otherwise the player who called out the last word or phrase, that no one could follow, drops out. In either case, the next player starts another round with a fresh word or phrase. The last player left in is the winner.

Here is an example of how a game with four players might start:

Player 1:	Brief Case
Player 2:	Casebook
Player 3:	Bookmark
Player 4:	Mark Time
Player 1:	Timepiece
Player 2:	Piece Work
Player 3:	Work Place
Player 4:	Place Setting
Player 1:	Setting Sun
Player 2:	Sunspot

Performance Games

Peculiar Leader

Despite its name, this game has nothing to do with politics. It is a parlour game in which you as the leader get up and tell the other players what you do and don't like. Whenever one of the players feels he has caught on to the reason *why* you like this but you don't like that, he puts up his hand and gives an example of what he thinks you do and don't like. If he has indeed caught onto the gist of your peculiar likes and dislikes, congratulate him. The last player to put up his hand and show he has grasped the nature of your likes and dislikes is the loser.

See how long it takes you to discover why one thing is liked and another disliked in this list of examples:

I like coffee but I don't like tea.
I like trees but I don't like flowers.
I like yellow but I don't like blue.
I like balloons but I don't like party hats.
I like butterflies but I don't like moths.
I like bees but I don't like ants.
I like boots but I don't like shoes.
I like spoons but I don't like forks.
I like doors but I don't like windows.
I like swimmers but I don't like divers.
I like football but I don't like boxing.

As you no doubt guessed by the second or third example, the items I like all included double letters in their spelling.

Here is a different set of likes and dislikes, this one perhaps more difficult to catch on to than the last:

I like ants but I don't like bees.
I like the stupid but I don't like the wise.
I like beans but I don't like peas.
I like noses but I don't like eyes.
I like hard work but I don't like ease.
I like coffee but I don't like tea.
I like sheep but I don't like ewes.
I like lakes but I don't like the sea.
I like me but I don't like you.

Here all the things I don't like sound like letters of the alphabet: B's, Y's, P's, I's, E's, T, U's, C, U.

When playing the game with a group of three or more, the loser of one round should be the leader of the next and should think up his own formula for what he likes and dislikes.

Taboo

A very common word – like 'I' or 'and' or 'the' or 'this' or 'that' – is declared taboo and must not be spoken by any of the players. The leader of the group questions each player in turn, and any player uttering the forbidden word drops out. The last player left answering questions is the winner.

Forbidden Letter

This game is similar to TABOO, but a particular letter of the alphabet is banned, and the players must reply to the questions without using any word that contains the forbidden letter.

Tongue-Twisters

Each player is given a tongue-twister and just one minute in which to repeat it as many times as possible. An impartial observer is found to keep an eye on the stopwatch and an ear on the tongue-twisters, and the player who manages to cram the greatest number of correctly spoken twisters into his sixty seconds is the winner.

'The sixth sick sheik's sixth sheep's sick' is supposed to be the most difficult tongue-twister in the English language, but there are plenty of others that are simpler but just as much fun:

Truly rural.
Lemon liniment.
Cricket critic.
Preshrunk shirts.
Red lorry, yellow lorry.
Strange strategic statistics.
Twine three tree twigs.

Six slim slender saplings.
That bloke's back brake-block broke.
She sells sea-shells on the sea-shore.
The minx mixed a medicinal mixture.
They threw three thick things at three thrilled thrushes.
Frisky Freddy feeds on fresh fried fish.
The city sweep shook his sooty sheet in the city street.
Whistle for the thistle sifter.
Around the rugged rocks the ragged rascal ran.
Shiver and slither shovelling slushy squelchy snow.
The Swiss witch which bewitched this switch wished the switch
bewitched.

Yarn-Spinning

This is one of those games that only works if someone has taken the
trouble to prepare it properly. All you need to do is fill a cardboard box
with a random selection of different and preferably slightly eccentric
objects. For example: a revolver, a railway timetable, a jar of peanut
butter, an egg-timer, some dice, a bible, a Mickey Mouse watch, a red
flag, a broken telescope, a plant, some sweets, a foreign stamp and an
empty toothpaste tube would do very nicely.

To play the game invite each player in turn to close his eyes and pick
four objects out of the box. You then give him five minutes in which to
tell a story, any story he cares to invent – the only condition being that he
must bring each of his four objects into that story at some stage. When
everyone has spun their yarn, the player who is considered to have told
the most effective and entertaining tale is declared the winner.

Hobbies

The question-master prepares a list of names of famous people. This may
be done mentally or with pencil and paper. Let us suppose the list begins
with Ronald Reagan, Mia Farrow and Peter Sellers. The question-master
then asks each player in turn, 'What's your hobby?', using one of the
names on the list.

For example, he says to the first player, 'What's your hobby, Ronald
Reagan?' to which that player, quick as a flash, must return an answer
like 'Running races' or 'Reading romances' or any other answer in which
the initial letters are the same as the name being used.

The second player is asked, 'What's your hobby, Mia Farrow?' and must immediately give a reply such as 'Making films' or 'Mending fences'.

The third player, having been asked, 'What's your hobby, Peter Sellers?' might reply without hesitation 'Playing snooker' or 'Polishing shoes'.

Any player who fails to give an appropriate reply (almost) immediately drops out. The last player left in the game is the winner.

Favourite Foods

FAVOURITE FOODS is an amusing variation of HOBBIES. The rules are the same but the question this time is 'What is your favourite food?'
Let's have a demonstration:

'What's your favourite food, Ronald Reagan?' 'Roast radishes.'
'What's your favourite food, Mia Farrow?' 'Mouse fillets.'
'What's your favourite food, Peter Sellers?' 'Pickled sausages.'
'What's your favourite food, Frank Sinatra?' 'Fried spaghetti.'
'What's your favourite food, Gyles Brandreth?' 'Gooey bananas.'

Coffee Pot

One player thinks of a word that has two or more meanings (e.g. Row) or a pair of words which have different meanings but which sound the same (e.g. Band and Banned). He then says aloud a sentence using both meanings but substituting the words 'coffee pot' for both of them – for example, 'I passed a coffee pot of trees as I was going for a coffee pot on the river' or 'The coffee pot was so rowdy that it was coffee pot from appearing again at the theatre.'

Each of the other players may then ask one question, and the first player's answer must include one or other of his words, or his word in one or another of its senses, again disguised as 'coffee pot'.

A player who manages to identify the 'coffee pot' word scores one point, otherwise the player who thought of the word scores the point. Each player takes it in turn to think of a 'coffee pot' word, and when everyone has had a go the player with the highest number of points is the winner.

Just A Minute

Players take it in turn to talk on a set subject for just a minute. They start with ten points apiece and when they have been talking for sixty seconds, without hesitating, repeating themselves or deviating from the subject, they are awarded another five points. However, if they *are* guilty of hesitation, repetition or deviation they *lose* two points. Before the game starts an impartial observer should be chosen to choose the subjects for discourse, impose the penalties and keep the score. Some examples of suitable topics are:

> A Visit To The Theatre
> Crossing The Atlantic
> The Decline And Fall Of The Roman Empire
> A Stitch In Time Saves Nine
> If I Ruled The World
> The Changing Seasons

What Nonsense!

This game is similar to JUST A MINUTE – the difference is that the topics chosen are so ridiculous that only the best performers can speak on them for sixty seconds without hesitation, repetition or deviation. For example:

> I Was A Teenage Taxidermist
> The Do-It-Yourself Heart Transplant
> Werewolves I Have Met
> The Differences Between Chalk And Cheese
> Earthworm Farming In Mongolia

Balderdash

Whereas the topics in the previous game were ridiculous, the topics on which the performers have to expound in BALDERDASH are completely meaningless. Furthermore, they have to speak for two whole minutes on topics such as:

> If I Am Here, Where Is Thursday?
> How To Eat The Moon

The Cosmic Significance Of Custard
The Answer That Cannot Be Questioned
Algebra Versus Chicago And Why Not
If But Was
The Inverse Functionalism Of Sybaritic Dichotomy

This game is to be attempted only by those with the readiest of wits and the most fluent of tongues.

Shrewd Simon Short

This is the ideal game for a party when everyone has had a few drinks. The idea is to see who can read the following passage out loud in the shortest time without hesitating or stumbling over the words.

Shrewd Simon Short sewed shoes. Seventeen summers, speeding storms, spreading sunshine successively, saw Simon's small, shabby shop still standing staunch, saw Simon's selfsame squeaking sign still swinging silently, specifying:

SIMON SHORT, SMITHFIELD'S SOLE SURVIVING SHOEMAKER.
SHOES SEWED, SOLED SUPERFINELY.

Simon's spry, sedulous spouse, Sally Short, sewed shirts, stitched sheets, stuffed sofas. Simon's six stout sons – Seth, Samuel, Stephen, Saul, Silas, Shadrach – sold sundries. Sober Seth sold sugar, spices; simple Sam sold saddles, stirrups, screws; sagacious Stephen sold silks, satins, shawls; sceptical Saul sold silver salvers; selfish Shadrach sold salves, shoestrings, soap, saws, skates; slack Silas sold Sally Short's stuffed sofas.

Some seven summers since, Simon's second son Samuel saw Sophia Sophronia Spriggs somewhere. Sweet, smart, sensible Sophia Sophronia Spriggs. Sam soon showed strong symptoms. Sam seldom stayed storing, selling saddles. Sam sighed sorrowfully, sought Sophia Sophronia's society, sang several serenades slyly. Simon stormed, scolded severely, said Sam seemed so silly singing such shameful, senseless songs. 'Strange Sam should slight such splendid sales! Strutting spendthrift! Scatter-brained simpleton!'

'Softly, softly, sire,' said Sally. 'Sam's smitten; Sam's spied some sweetheart.'

'Sentimental schoolboy!' snarled Simon. 'Smitten! Stop such stuff.' Simon sent Sally's snuffbox spinning, seized Sally's

scissors, smashed Sally's spectacles, scattering several spools,
'Sneaking scoundrel! Sam's shocking silliness shall surcease!'
Scowling, Simon stopped speaking, started swiftly shopward.
Sally sighed sadly. Summoning Sam, she spoke sweet sym-
pathy. 'Sam,' said she, 'sire seems singularly snappy; so, solicit,
sue, secure Sophronia speedily, Sam.'
'So soon? So soon?' said Sam, standing stock-still.
'So soon, surely,' said Sally, smiling, 'specially since sire
shows such spirits.'
So Sam, somewhat scared, sauntered slowly, shaking
stupendously. Sam soliloquized: 'Sophia Sophronia Spriggs,
Spriggs — Short — Sophia Sophronia Short — Samuel Short's
spouse — sounds splendid! Suppose she should say — she shan't
— she shan't!'
Soon Sam spied Sophia starching shirts, singing softly.
Seeing Sam, she stopped starching, saluting Sam smilingly.
Sam stammered shockingly.
'Spl-spl-splendid summer season, Sophia.'
'Selling saddles still, Sam?'
'Sar-sar-tin,' Sam, starting suddenly. 'Season's somewhat
soporific,' said Sam, steadily staunching streaming sweat,
shaking sensibly.
'Sartin,' said Sophia, smiling significantly.
'Sip some sweet sherbert, Sam.' (Silence, sixty seconds.)
'Sire shot sixty sheldrakes, Saturday,' said Sophia.
'Sixty? Shot!' said Sam. (Silence seventy-seven seconds.)
'See sister Susan's sunflowers,' said Sophia socially, stop-
ping such stiff silence.
Sophia's sprightly sauciness stimulated Sam strangely: so
Sam suddenly spoke sentimentally: 'Sophia, Susan's
sunflowers seem saying Samuel Short, Sophia Sophronia
Spriggs, stroll serenely, seek some sequestered spot, some
sylvan shade. Sparkling springs shall sing soul-stirring strains;
Sweet songsters shall silence secret sighings; super-angelic
sylphs shall — ' Sophia snickered; so Sam stopped.
'Sophia,' said Sam solemnly.
'Sam,' said Sophia.
'Sophia, stop smiling; Sam Short's sincere. Sam's seeking
some sweet spouse, Sophia.'
Sophia stood silent.
'Speak, Sophia, speak; such suspense speculates sorrow.'
'Seek sire, Sam, seek sire.'
So Sam sought sire Spriggs; sire Spriggs said, 'Sartin.'

As reading this passage faultlessly from beginning to end is an almost impossible task, each player may be allowed to correct up to three mistakes before being disqualified. If none of the players manages to complete the passage, the winner will be the player who read most of the passage before being disqualified.

Games For Two

Yes No

Player One barrages Player Two with quick-fire questions, to which
Player Two must reply without hesitation and without using the words
Yes and No. For example:

STAN:	'Are you ready to start?'
OLIVER:	'I certainly am.'
STAN:	'You didn't nod your head, did you?'
OLIVER:	'I did not.'
STAN:	'Have you had your holiday this year?'
OLIVER:	'I have.'
STAN:	'Did you go abroad?'
OLIVER:	'That is so.'
STAN:	'You didn't hesitate just then, did you?'
OLIVER:	'Certainly not.'
STAN:	'Are you sure.'
OLIVER:	'Sure.'

Player Two wins if he can survive this interrogation for sixty seconds without using the words Yes or No, otherwise Player One wins.
The players then change roles for another round.

Messing About In Quotes

One player comes up with a well-known phrase or quotation or cliché,
and the other player has to suggest who might have said it. The players
then swap roles. Nobody is awarded any points, penalties or prizes, but
with quick-witted players the game can be a joy. To set you going, who
said, 'Thank God it's Friday'? Why, Robinson Crusoe, of course!

Crambo

All the great masters of English literature have enjoyed the occasional
game of CRAMBO. To play it, one player thinks of a word and announces

a word that rhymes with the secret word he has thought of. The other players are then allowed three attempts at guessing the word. If a player guesses the word correctly he has the honour of choosing the word for the next round. If none of the other players can guess the word or if they have all fallen asleep, the original player has another turn.

Stinkety Pinkety

In STINKETY PINKETY each player in turn offers a definition which the other player must translate into a noun followed by a rhyming adjective.
For example:

Definition:	An obese feline.
Answer:	Fat cat.
Definition:	A very unmelodious group of singers.
Answer:	Dire choir.
Definition:	A cowardly shout.
Answer:	Yellow bellow.
Definition:	A comparatively tranquil agriculturist.
Answer:	Calmer farmer.
Definition:	A cactus in a bad mood.
Answer:	Truculent succulent.
Definition:	A self-denying art-lover.
Answer:	Aesthetic ascetic.

(To connoisseurs of this game, an example using monosyllabic adjective and noun is known as a Stink Pink, with two syllables a Stinky Pinky, and with three syllables a Stinkety Pinkety.)

Proverbs

Player One chooses a secret proverb and tells Player Two the number of words it contains. Player Two has to guess the secret proverb by asking a series of questions, which may be about any subject under the sun. He gets his clues because Player One must include the first word of his proverb in his answer to the first question, the second word in his answer to the second question, and so, until all the words in the secret proverb have been accounted for.

With 'Too many cooks spoil the broth' as the secret proverb, the questioning might go something like this:

MATTHEW: 'Does this proverb express a basic truth about life?'
ARNOLD: 'Yes, definitely. If anything, I'd say it's almost *too* true.'
MATTHEW: 'How old are you?'
ARNOLD: 'So *many* years have passed since I was born that I'm afraid I have lost count.'
MATTHEW: 'What is your favourite colour?'
ARNOLD: 'Well, I like the red jackets worn by guardsmen, the white hats worn by *cooks*, and the black boots worn by policemen.'
MATTHEW: 'Where are you going for your holiday this year?'
ARNOLD: 'Oh, I think it would *spoil* the game if I gave you a straight answer to that question.'
MATTHEW: 'OK, back to the proverb – is it very well known?'
ARNOLD: 'Oh yes, I would say it is one of *the* most popular proverbs.'
MATTHEW: 'When did you first hear this proverb?'
ARNOLD: 'Oh, years ago, some old farmer told it to me over a dinner of chicken *broth*, meat balls and boiled cabbage.'

The crafty player will include in his answers plenty of red herrings, such as 'eggs', 'basket', 'cloud', 'lining', 'look', 'leap', etc.

The Railway Carriage Game

Two players are chosen and each of them is given a secret (and slightly absurd) phrase, sentence or expression. For example, the first player's phrase could be 'Pigs might fly' while the second player's phrase might be 'I did it my way'. Armed with their phrases, the players must climb into an imaginary railway carriage and chat to one another for the length of a two-minute journey. During the course of their conversation each player must slip his or her secret phrase into whatever he or she happens to say. It isn't easy – particularly when you remember that the aim of the game is to introduce your secret phrase without your opponent realizing you have done so.

When the journey is over, the first player must attempt to guess the identity of the second player's phrase, and vice-versa.

Questions! Questions!

In QUESTIONS! QUESTIONS! the first player begins with a question, his opponent must reply with another question, the first player puts a third question, the opponent responds with a fourth, and so on, until one of the players falters or forgets himself and fails to ask a question. Repetition is not allowed.

To give you a better idea of how the game can go, here is a brief bout between Lewis and Carol:

LEWIS:	What time is it?
CAROL:	Why do you want to know?
LEWIS:	Why do you ask that?
CAROL:	Why can't you answer a civil question?
LEWIS:	Why can't you look at your watch?
CAROL:	When are you going to get yourself a watch?
LEWIS:	What's that got to do with it?
CAROL:	Who do you think you are talking to me like that?
LEWIS:	Where can I find someone who will tell me the time?
CAROL:	Where can I find a husband who can afford a watch of his own?
LEWIS:	When do you stop nagging?
CAROL:	Why don't you stop going on like this?
LEWIS:	Do you know something?
CAROL:	What?
LEWIS:	Do you know who you remind me of?
CAROL:	Who?
LEWIS:	Your mother!

Lewis managed to get his insult in, but he lost the game.

If you want to see how the game can be played at its most brilliant, get hold of a copy of Tom Stoppard's play *Rosencrantz and Guildenstern Are Dead*. The two characters play this game in the play and do so with breathtaking verve.

Ghost

There are few games as good as GHOST for sorting out those with impressive vocabularies from those without. It is a word game for two players in which they build up a series of letters to form a word but endeavour not to be the player that completes a word.

The first player begins by calling out a letter. The second player adds a second letter to the first, making sure that the two-letter combination could actually begin a valid word. The first player adds a third letter, again thinking of a valid word that begins with that letter combination. The second player adds a fourth letter, and so it goes on – until one of the players is forced to complete a word, in which case that player has lost the game.

Players must at all times have a valid word in mind, and one player may challenge the other if he feels that his opponent did not have a valid word in mind. If the challenged player cannot produce an acceptable word, he loses the round. If the challenged player, however, can produce an acceptable word, then it is the challenger who loses the round.

By the way, it is only when a word of four or more letters is completed that a player loses if he completes a word. If this rule did not apply, the range of possible openings to the game would be severely limited – no word, for example, beginning with HA, HE, HI, or HO.

Here is an example:

HENRY:	G. (He is thinking of GARDEN)
JAMES:	G-r. (He is thinking of GREAT)
HENRY:	G-r-a. (He is thinking of GRADUATE)
JAMES:	G-r-a-n. (He is thinking of GRAND or GRANT)
HENRY:	G-r-a-n-u. (He is now thinking of GRANULAR)
JAMES:	G-r-a-n-u-l. (He is thinking of GRANULE)
HENRY:	G-r-a-n-u-l-a. (Still thinking of GRANULAR)
JAMES:	G-r-a-n-u-l-a-t. (Thinking of GRANULATE).
HENRY:	G-r-a-n-u-l-a-t-e. (Henry loses the round)

Superghost

SUPERGHOST is GHOST for masterminds. The principle of the game is the same. The difference is that in SUPERGHOST players may add their letters to either end of the group of letters as it is being built up! It requires a high degree of mental agility as well as an impressive vocabulary, as can be seen in this example:

JAMES:	R. (He is thinking of RACK)
JOYCE:	R-o. (She is thinking of ROBOT)
JAMES:	T-r-o. (He is thinking of TROUBLE)
JOYCE:	N-t-r-o. (She is thinking of INTRODUCE)
JAMES:	O-n-t-r-o. (Thinking of CONTROVERT)
JOYCE:	C-o-n-t-r-o. (Thinking of CONTROL)
JAMES:	N-c-o-n-t-r-o. (Thinking of UNCONTROLLED)

JOYCE:	N-c-o-n-t-r-o-v. (Thinking of UNCONTROVERSIAL)
JAMES:	N-c-o-n-t-r-o-v-e. (Also thinking of UNCONTROVERSIAL)
JOYCE:	N-c-o-n-t-r-o-v-e-r. (Still thinking of UNCONTROVERSIAL)
JAMES:	I-n-c-o-n-t-r-o-v-e-r. (Realizing that with UNCONTROVERSIAL he will lose the round, he has thought of INCONTROVERTIBLE)
JOYCE:	I-n-c-o-n-t-r-o-v-e-r-t. (Unable to think of any alternative, she faces the prospect of imminent defeat)
JAMES:	I-n-c-o-n-t-r-o-v-e-r-t-i.
JOYCE:	I-n-c-o-n-t-r-o-v-e-r-t-i-b.
JAMES:	I-n-c-o-n-t-r-o-v-e-r-t-i-b-l.
JOYCE:	I-n-c-o-n-t-r-o-v-e-r-t-i-b-l-e.

Guessing Games

Dumb Crambo

Two teams are formed. Team A goes out of the room, while the members of team B confer among themselves to choose a mystery word. Once the word is chosen, team A returns and team B announces a word that rhymes with the word they have chosen.

Team A must now try to guess the mystery word. However, they are not allowed to speak – they must act out their guesses in dumb-show. Any player who speaks automatically loses the games for his team. Incorrect guesses are greeted with boos and hisses; correct guesses are greeted with applause and the successful team gains a point.

When the secret word has been guessed, or when teams A has made three incorrect guesses, the teams change roles for another round. The team with the most points after a pre-determined number of rounds is the winner.

Aesop's Mission

A player who is in the know plays the part of Aesop. Having secretly picked on a letter of the alphabet that is to be taboo, Aesop proceeds to ask a series of questions of the other players. If a player's reply contains the forbidden letter Aesop says 'Bad!', otherwise he says 'Good!'

Let's suppose the letter L is taboo.

AESOP (to JOHN):	'How old are you?'
JOHN:	'Twenty-three.'
AESOP:	'Good!'
AESOP (to George):	'How old are you?'
GEORGE:	'Eleven.'
AESOP:	'Bad!'
AESOP (to PAUL):	'Where did you go at the weekend?'
PAUL:	'Liverpool.'
AESOP:	'Bad!'
AESOP (to RINGO):	'What did you have for lunch today?'
RINGO:	'A hamburger.'
AESOP:	'Good!'

Those players who have encountered the game before have to try to work out what the taboo is; the others have first to try to work out what game is all about.

Clue Words

The questioner thinks of a mystery word containing seven letters with no letters duplicated. The other players have to try to guess the mystery word with the help of up to three clues.

The first clue is a three-letter word formed from three letters in the mystery word. Each player is allowed one guess at the mystery word. A successful guess is worth 3 points, but there is no penalty for failure.

If no one has guessed the word, the questioner gives a second clue. This is a four-letter word using letters in the mystery word. Again each player is allowed one guess, and correctly guessing the mystery word is now worth 2 points.

If the mystery word is still unguessed, the questioner gives the third clue, which is a five-letter word formed from letters in the mystery word. Each player again has one guess and if correct earns 1 point.

If a player guesses the mystery word at any stage he takes a turn as questioner for the next round. If no one has guessed correctly after the three clues have been given, the questioner scores one point and has another turn.

The player with the highest number of points, after an agreed number of rounds, is the winner.

How easy it is to guess the mystery word depends on how much information the questioner gives away in his clues. Let's say the mystery word is *coaster*. Clues of *act*, *cart* and *cater* leave two letters still undisclosed. But if clue 1 is *act* and clue 2 is *rose*, all the letters have been revealed and the word should be easily guessed.

Twenty Questions

One player thinks of an object – which may be anything from a dinosaur to Mickey Mouse's left shoe, from a tomato to a battleship – and announces whether it is Animal, Vegetable, Mineral or any combination thereof. The other players then fire questions which require only 'Yes' or 'No' answers and which are aimed at narrowing the field and eventually closing in on the mystery object. Only twenty questions are allowed, and if the mystery object has not been identified when twenty questions have been asked, the player who thought of it has won and chooses another mystery object.

Virginia Woolf

This is a variation of TWENTY QUESTIONS. All the players have to think of the person they would most like to be if they couldn't be themselves. You can choose to be a character from fact or fiction, alive or dead, male or female, but you should be someone whose name the other players are likely to know.

When everyone has chosen his or her ideal identity, each player takes it in turn to be quizzed by the remaining players whose aim it is to find out who the player in question would like to be. Twenty questions are allowed, requiring either 'Yes' or 'No' answers. When the secret identity has been revealed, the player whose choice it was must explain *why* he wanted to be whoever it was he happened to choose.

Where Am I?

In this variation of TWENTY QUESTIONS one player thinks of a place and an activity he might be doing there and then asks 'Where am I?'. The other players then have twenty questions, requiring 'Yes' or 'No' answers, to determine where the player has imagined himself to be and what it is he has imagined himself to be doing there.

Charades

CHARADES is a very popular game in which one team of players has to guess a word of several syllables presented in dramatic form by the other team.

The players divide into teams, and the first team disappears to another room to choose the word it is going to dramatize and to work out exactly how it is going to set about it. The word that is chosen must be of several syllables, and each part of the word must lend itself to dramatization, as must the word as a whole. Only the sound of the syllables or component parts of the word matters, not the spelling.

The word and the manner of presentation having been decided upon, the captain of the team returns and announces to the opposing team how many syllables there are in the word his team has chosen. Various members of the team then come into the room and act, with or without dialogue (it is far more entertaining without), a series of scenes designed to give clues to the sounds of the syllables they are dramatizing. Each syllable is acted out individually and finally the word is performed as a whole.

When the opposing team have guessed the word being presented it becomes their turn to leave the room and decide on a charade.

A variation of traditional CHARADES that has become quite as popular as the original involves the performers in dramatizing not merely an everyday word, but the name of a famous person, town, country, etc., or the title of a book, play, film or song. When this form of the game is played, the titles are normally broken down into individual words rather than syllables.

Another variation is SOLO CHARADES, in which individual players, rather than teams, take it in turn to perform the words or titles they choose.

If you would like to play CHARADES, but are stuck for ideas, here are a few suggestions, all of which should lend themselves to entertaining presentation:

abandon (a, band, don)
acrostic (a, cross, tic)
archery (arch, cherry)
assault (ass, salt)
barbecue (barber, cue)
bedlam (bed, lamb)
butterfly (butt, her, fly)
cabbage (cab, age)
caribou (carry, boo)
carnival (car, navel)
chauffeur (show, fur)
classic (class, sick)
correct (core, wrecked)
cucumber (queue, come, burr)
dinosaur (die, nose, sore)
discontent (disc, corn, tent)
domestic (dough, mess, stick)
dynamite (dine, aim, mite)
elastic (eel, last, tick)
excursion (eggs, cur, shun)
fahrenheit (far, wren, height)
fertilize (fur, till, eyes)
foreleg (fall, egg)

fundamental (fun, dam, mental)
grocer (gross, sir)
hallucination (halo, sin, nation)
harpsichord (harp, sick, cord)
holidays (holly, daze)
horizon (whore, rise, sun)
hospitality (horse, spit, alley, tea)
hydraulic (high, draw, lick)
hypnotic (hip, knot, tic)
illustrate (ill, lust, straight)
industry (in, dust, tree)
intelligence (in, telly, gents)
jasmine (jazz, mine)
khaki (car, key)
kidney (kid, knee)
lacrosse (lack, cross)
legionnaire (lee, John, air)
manicure (man, nick, cure)
manipulate (man, nip, you, late)
metronome (met, row, gnome)
misanthropy (miss, sand, throw,
   pea)
misunderstand (miss, under, stand)

mosquito (moss, key, toe)
navigator (navvy, gaiter)
nightingale (knight, tin, gale)
Olympics (o, limp, picks)
origin (awe, ridge, gin)
panorama (pan, or, armour)
pendulum (pen, duel, hum)
philosopher (fill, loss, offer)
psychology (sigh, collar, gee)
relief (reel, leaf)
renegade (wren, egg, aid)
robust (row, bust)
romantic (roam, antic)
sacrifice (sack, reef, ice)
sentry (scent, tree)
succeed (suck, seed)
telegram (tell, leg, ram)
trapeze (trap, ease)
universe (you, knee, verse)
valiant (valley, ant)
vampire (vamp, higher)
waitress (weight, tress)
waterfall (war, turf, all)
wholesaler (hole, sailor)
window (win, dough)
wonderful (one dare, full)

The African Queen
All Quiet On The Western Front
Blowin' In The Wind
The Blue Angel
Brave New World
Bridge Over Troubled Water
A Bridge Too Far
Carousel
Crime And Punishment
Duck Soup
Everything You Always Wanted
    To Know About Sex But Were
    Afraid To Ask

Far From The Madding Crowd
Fiddler On The Roof
A Fistful Of Dollars
From Russia With Love
The Good, The Bad And The
    Ugly
Great Expectations
Heart Of Glass
Horse Feathers
I'm Dreaming Of A White
    Christmas
The Jewel In The Crown
The King And I
Little Big Man
Look Back In Anger
Lord Of The Flies
Lord Of The Rings
The Man In The Iron Mask
Midnight Cowboy
My Fair Lady
The Naked And The Dead
One Flew Over The Cuckoo's
    Nest
Over The Rainbow
The Owl And The Pussycat
Penny Lane
Pop Goes The Weasel
River Deep, Mountain High
Rock Around The Clock
Sergeant Pepper's Lonely Hearts
    Club Band
Seven Brides For Seven Brothers
Silent Night
Star Wars
The Sting
Straw Dogs
The Taming Of The Shrew
Tie A Yellow Ribbon
Watership Down
What's My Line?

Botticelli

One player thinks of the name of a famous person or a well-known character from fiction. He reveals the first letter of his chosen subject's surname to the company, who must then try to discover who it is the player is thinking of.

They go about this task by asking the player two types of question: indirect and direct. They can only ask a direct question if the player has failed to come up with a satisfactory answer to an indirect question. For example, if the player chooses to be Winston Churchill, he will announce 'I am someone beginning with C', and the others will proceed to fire indirect questions at him, such as 'Are you a French painter?', 'Are you a castaway?' The player must reply along these lines: 'No, I am not Cezanne' or 'No, I am not Robinson Crusoe'. If he cannot think of appropriate answers, because he does not know of a French painter or a castaway beginning with C, or because his mind has gone blank at the crucial moment, the questioner can then ask a direct question – 'Are you alive?', 'Are you fictional?', 'Are you Norwegian?' – to which a truthful 'Yes' or 'No' answer must be given. It is important, therefore, that the player chooses a character about whom he has some knowledge, or he may not be able to give correct answers to the direct questions.

Naturally, the questioners must do their best to ask awkward indirect questions in order to get as many opportunities as possible to put direct questions, which will lead them eventually to the secret identity they're after. The questioners can corner the player in one of two ways: either by asking an indirect question – 'Were you born in 1874 and were you Prime Minister of Britain between 1940 and 1945?' – which forces the player to reveal his identity, or by asking a direct question – 'Are you Winston Churchill?' – where the player has no alternative but to say 'Yes'.

Kolodny's Game

KOLODNY'S GAME is a rather strange game of induction. The players have to ask questions that can be answered with a 'Yes' or a 'No' and have to guess, from the answers, what the secret rule is that determines what the answers should be. Is that perfectly clear? No? Well, let's look at the start of a typical game, played by three players – Peter, Paul and Mary.

Peter decides on a secret rule that has to be discovered by Paul and Mary. The rule he chooses is: If the question consists of more than five words then the answer is 'Yes', otherwise the answer is 'No'. This is typical of the sort of rule used in the game. Here are a few more examples:

(a) If the question begins with the word 'Is' the answer is 'Yes', otherwise the answer is 'No'.

(b) If the age of the questioner is less than 25 the answer is 'Yes', otherwise the answer is 'No'.

(c) If the last letter of the question is in the first half of the alphabet the answer is 'Yes', if it is in the second half the answer is 'No'.

Paul and Mary now start asking questions:

'Are you stupid?' 'No.'
'Is anyone in this room stupid?' 'Yes.'
'Do you have a problem sleeping at night?' 'Yes.'
'Have you tried counting sheep?' 'No.'
'Is this an easy rule to guess?' 'Yes.'

Note that the actual meaning of the questions is irrelevant – it is the form of the question that is significant. The way to play successfully is to try to work out what the questions answered 'Yes' might have in common that is not shared by the questions answered 'No' (and vice versa), to form hypotheses, and to frame questions designed to test out your hypotheses.

For example, from the questions and answers above, you might form the hypothesis that the rule is: Questions starting with a two-letter word are answered 'Yes'. But if, to test your theory, you then ask 'Is coal black?' you will get the answer 'No', disproving the theory, so you will have to think again.

Alphabet And List Games

The Zoo Game

The first player names an animal beginning with A, and then starts counting to ten. Before he reaches ten, the next player must name a different animal beginning with A and start counting to ten. Before he reaches ten, the next player must name a different animal beginning with A, and so on until a player fails to come up with a name before he is counted out or until a player repeats a name that has already been used. That player drops out. The next player starts again with the name of an animal beginning with B.

For example, with four players the game might proceed like this:

MATTHEW:	'Ape. One, two, three . . .'
MARK:	'Alligator. One, two, three, four, five, six . . .'
LUKE:	'Antelope. One, two, three, four . . .'
JOHN:	Ass. One, two, three . . .'
MATTHEW:	'Aardvark. One, two, three, four, five, six, seven, eight, nine, ten.'

Mark is out, as he could not think of another animal beginning with A (such as armadillo, ant-eater, aurochs, addax, agouti, ai, anoa, argali, aye-aye, acouchy, angwantibo or amon).

LUKE:	'Bear. One, two, three, four . . .'
JOHN:	'Buffalo. One, two . . .'
MATTHEW:	'Beaver. One, two, three . . .'
LUKE:	'Badger. One, two, three, four, five . . .'
JOHN:	'Bison. One, two, three, four, five, six, seven, eight, nine . . .'
MATTHEW (in desperation):	'Bear. One, two . . .'

Matthew is out, as 'bear' has already been used.

LUKE:	'Cat. One, two, three . . .'
JOHN:	'Cow. One, two, three, four . . .'
LUKE:	'Camel. One, two . . .'
JOHN:	'Chimpanzee. One, two, three, four . . .'
LUKE:	'Coyote. One, two, three, four, five, six, seven, eight, nine, ten.'

John is counted out before he can think of another name, so Luke is the winner.

When you are tired of animals, you can play the game with some other category: Birds, Composers, Rivers, or whatever.

The Preacher's Cat

The first player starts the game by declaring 'The preacher's cat is an amiable cat and his name is Archibald'. The next player then suggests, 'The preacher's cat is an amorous cat and his name is Andrew'. The third player avers, 'The preacher's cat is an abhorrent cat and his name is Alexander'. And so it goes on around the group until all the players have come up with an adjective and a name beginning with A.

Then they must each in turn find adjectives and names beginning with B, then with C, and so on, until they get to the fact that 'The preacher's cat is a zealous cat and his name is Zebediah'. The letters Q and X may be omitted, but anyone failing to come up with an adjective or name for any other letter drops out.

Traveller's Alphabet

The players sit in a circle and each player in turn asks the person on his left two questions: 'Where are you going?' and 'What will you do there?'. The replies consist of the name of a country and the description of an activity, using verb, adjective and noun – all beginning with the same letter of the alphabet. The first player's replies must begin with the letter A, the second player's with B, the third player's with C, and so on.

For example, a game might begin like this:

CHARLES:	'Where are you going?'
EDWARD:	'Algeria.'
CHARLES:	'What will you do there?'
EDWARD:	'Assist Arab archaeologists.'
EDWARD:	'Where are you going?'
STUART:	'Belgium.'
EDWARD:	'What will you do there?'
STUART:	'Buy beer bottles.'
STUART:	'Where are you going?'
CHARLES:	'Canada.'

> STUART: 'What will you do there?'
> CHARLES: 'Catch crazy criminals.'

Any player failing to come up with an answer within a reasonable time is disqualified, and the last player left in is the winner.

Word Lightning

The question-master chooses a victim and gives him a letter. The hapless victim then has sixty seconds in which to rattle off as many words as he can start with the chosen letter. The question-master keeps count. When all the players have been given a letter and a minute to do their best, the player with the highest word count is the winner.

It sounds ridiculously easy when you read it in print, but when you're put on the spot it's another matter.

Letters By Numbers

This game is suitable for any small number of players and is a good test of how quick their thinking is.

The question-master calls out, at random, a series of numbers between one and twenty-six. For each number called out, the aim is to see which player can be first to respond with the letter at that position in the alphabet.

For example:

'Seventeen!'	'Q.'
'Five!'	'E.'
'Twenty-three!'	'W.'

The first player to respond correctly to each number scores one point. Any player naming the wrong letter loses a point. After the game has been played for an agreed length of time, the player with the highest score is the winner.

Vowels Out

The question-master gives each player in turn an equally long and equally difficult word to spell. All the players have to do is spell the words correctly, remembering, however, that they must not utter any of the five vowels. When they get to a vowel they must adopt a special sign language: to indicate an A you raise your right arm; to indicate an E you raise your left arm; to indicate an I you point to your own eye; to indicate an O you point to your mouth; and to indicate a U you point to the question-master.

Any player spelling a word incorrectly, uttering a vowel or mixing up the signals is disqualified. The last player left spelling is the winner.

Leading Lights

For this game you need to prepare a list of names of well-known people, living or dead. For each name on the list the players have to think of an appropriate phrase that characterizes or defines that name beginning with the same initial letters as the name in question.

For example, a player might come up with the following phrases:

Frank Sinatra	– Famous Singer
Wolfgang Amadeus Mozart	– Wrote Appealing Melodies
Brigitte Bardot	– Beautiful Body
Albert Einstein	– Atomic Energy
William Shakespeare	– Wrote Sonnets
Paul McCartney	– Popular Musician

Games For Children And Others

I Went To Market

This game is suitable for younger children, and is educational in that it helps the children to learn the alphabet. Despite being educational, it is very popular with children!

The players have to think of nouns beginning with each letter of the alphabet in turn to complete the sentence 'I went to market and I bought . . .'.

For example:

> Player 1: 'I went to market and I bought apples.'
> Player 2: 'I went to market and I bought books.'
> Player 3: 'I went to market and I bought cabbages.'
> Player 4: 'I went to market and I bought dolls.'

Difficult letters like K, Q, X, and Z may be omitted. If you get to the end of the alphabet, the next player starts again with A, but words used previously must not be repeated.

A Was An Apple Pie

This game is similar to I WENT TO MARKET except that the players have to supply verbs for each letter of the alphabet in turn. Player 1 starts: 'A was an apple pie. A ate it'. The game might then proceed: 'B bought it', 'C cut it', 'D delivered it', 'E examined it', and so on through the alphabet. There is no need to repeat the first phrase 'A was an apple pie' each time.

I Packed My Bag

In this well-known memory game the players have to remember and repeat an ever-increasing list of items.

The game starts with one player saying, for example, 'I packed my bag and in it I put a pair of pyjamas.' The second player repeats the sentence and adds another item of his own. The third player does likewise, adding a further item. And so it goes on, each player in turn repeating the list and adding one more item.

For example:

Player 1: 'I packed my bag and in it I put a pair of pyjamas.'

Player 2: 'I packed my bag and in it I put a pair of pyjamas and a hard-boiled egg.'

Player 3: 'I packed my bag and in it I put a pair of pyjamas, a hard-boiled egg and a video recorder.'

Player 4: 'I packed my bag and in it I put a pair of pyjamas, a hard-boiled egg, a video recorder and a Mickey Mouse wristwatch.'

Player 1: 'I packed my bag and in it I put a pair of pyjamas, a hard-boiled egg, a video recorder, a Mickey Mouse wristwatch and a peanut butter sandwich.'

Player 2: 'I packed my bag and in it I put a pair of pyjamas, a hard-boiled egg, a video recorder, a Mickey Mouse wristwatch, a peanut butter sandwich and a compass.'

A player who forgets any of the items, or lists them in the wrong order, leaves the game. The winner is the last player left in the game.

I Spy

This must surely be the best-known and most popular word game for children.

One player starts the game by mentally selecting some object that is in his range of vision and announces its initial letter thus (assuming the initial letter is S): 'I spy with my little eye something beginning with S'. The other players have to guess the mystery object, and they can call out their guesses at any time – there is no requirement to play in turn.

'Sofa?'
'No.'
'Sandwich?'
'No.'
'Ceiling???'
'No!'
'Shoe?'
'No.'
'Sock?'
'Yes!'

The first player to guess correctly becomes the 'spy' in the next round.

Sausages

This is a silly game which relies for its effect on the inexplicable fact that the word *sausages* tends to make people laugh.

One of the players is chosen to be the victim, and the other players bombard him with questions. These should be personal questions about the victim, his family, school, teachers, holidays, favourite activities, etc. To every question the victim must reply simply 'Sausages' and must keep a perfectly straight face throughout, however ridiculous the answer sounds.

For example:

'What clothes do you wear in winter?' 'Sausages.'
'What do you like best at school?' 'Sausages.'
'What is your uncle's name?' 'Sausages.'
'What do you like watching on TV?' 'Sausages.'

The questioners may smile, laugh, giggle, chuckle, smirk or guffaw as much as they please, which makes it even harder for the victim to keep a straight face. When the victim betrays any sign of mirth – and even the hardiest cannot keep a straight face for long – he gives way to another victim.

Spelling Bee

One player is selected to be the question-master and calls out a word to each of the other players in turn, who must give the correct spelling of the word in question. For spelling a word correctly a player gets one point. At the end of the game, the player with most points is the winner.

For the game to be a success, it is important that the words to be spelled are suited to the ages and abilities of the players taking part. The question-master may use a prepared list of words to be spelled or may make up the list as he goes along – the former is normally preferable.

There are a number of possible variations, including the following:

Variation 1:   The game is played as described above except that a player who spells a word incorrectly drops out. The last player left in is the winner.

Variation 2:   A player spelling a word correctly is given another word to spell. He gets one point for each word spelled correctly and his turn ends only when he makes a mistake.

Variation 3: The players are divided into two teams, and the question-master offers a word to each player in turn, selecting each team alternately. If a player fails to spell a word correctly it is offered to that player's opposite number in the opposing team for a bonus point.

Action Spelling

This is a silly and amusing form of SPELLING BEE. It is played in the same way as that game except that in the spelling certain letters are not called out – instead, various actions are substituted. For example, it might be decreed that G should be represented by a growl, B by flapping one's arms, Y by scratching one's head, and so on. You can invent as many such actions to represent letters as you like, depending on how silly and how complicated you want the game to be.

Any player spelling a word incorrectly or failing to substitute the correct action for a letter loses a point or drops out of the game.

Spelling Round

The question-master calls out words to be spelled. Each word has to be spelled out around the circle of players, each player in turn calling out one letter of the word. For example, if the word in question was 'Parallel', the first player would call out 'P', the second 'A', the third 'R', and so on. Any player making a mistake or hesitating too long drops out. The last player left in is the winner.

Famous Fives

The question-master asks each player in turn to name five objects in a given category, each player being given a new category. For example, 'Name five ice hockey teams', 'Name five breeds of dog', 'Name five countries in Europe', 'Name five card games', 'Name five seaside towns', 'Name five Walt Disney films'.

Players score one point for each item named, with a bonus point for naming all five in a category, but they lose a point for each incorrect item.

The game ends when a pre-determined number of rounds have been played, and the player with the highest score is the winner.

Consonant Catalogue

This game is best if played with a stop-watch or, at least, a watch with a second hand. Each player in turn has to recite the alphabet from B to Z, leaving out all the vowels. The player who does so in the fastest time is the winner.

It's a simple idea, but the task is tricker than it seems. Try it and see!

I Want A Rhyme

This game is suitable for children of all ages, but may require an adult or older child to act as question-master.

The question-master says:

'I want a rhyme
In jolly quick time,
And the word I choose is: red'

The word, of course, does not have to be red – it can be any word that has a lot of other words that rhyme with it – *hat*, *mole*, *gate*, *pin*, *ride*, *clock*, *shoe*, etc. – but preferably not *wolf* or *orange*!

After the question-master has announced his word, each player in turn has to give a word that rhymes with it. So with red you might get *bed*, *head*, *led*, *fed*, *shed*, *bread*, *sled*, *wed*, *dread*, going round the players until one player fails to think of a word and has to drop out. The question-master then announces a new word for which the surviving players have to find rhymes. This continues until all but one of the players have been eliminated, the last surviving player being the winner.

Sentences

The game starts with one player choosing a word and announcing it to all the other players. Any word will do, but one with five or more letters makes for more fun.

Each player must then form a sentence consisting of words beginning with the letters of the given word. You can choose whether or not you make it a rule that the sentence must be connected in some way with the chosen word.

So, for example, if the chosen word was 'Games', suitable sentences would be:

'Girls and men enjoy sailing.'
'Golfers are meeting every Sunday.'
'Good archers make excellent soldiers.'

Chinese Whispers

The players sit in a circle, and the first player whispers a message into the ear of the player to the left; that player whispers the message into the ear of the player on his left, and so on around the circle until the message gets back to the player who started it. That player then declares out loud the original message and the message that came back to him. The two are usually widely different, causing much hilarity. After this, another player originates a message and the game continues until each player has had a turn.

For example, starting with the message 'Bring up the infantry, we are going to advance' you are quite likely to end up with 'Brick up the fruit tree, we are going to a dance'.

What Are We Shouting?

The players are divided into two teams. One team leaves the room to decide amongst themselves on a well-known phrase or saying. Film or television titles or names of books or songs are also acceptable. Ideally the phrase will consist of as many words as there are players in the team – in any case, there must not be more words than there are players. One word of the phrase is allotted to each player. Some players will have to share a word if there are fewer words than players.

The team then returns. Then all at the same time, after a count of three, they shout their words as loud as they can. The opposing team may, if they wish, ask for the shout to be repeated, but must then attempt to guess the phrase being shouted. If they guess wrongly, the other team has another go with a new phrase, but if they guess correctly it is their turn to choose and shout.

PART TWO
WRITTEN GAMES

Panel Games

Word Endings

Give all players a long list of word endings and let them race to see which one can be the first to find words that end with the given endings. You don't need to make the endings too obscure: the last three letters of a word invariably look a little unfamiliar when they are given without anything preceding them, and endings that are rare tend to slow down the game. Here are some examples of the types of ending that work well:

-don	-ask
-ppy	-ngs
-per	-eth
-the	-ket
-mum	-ssy
-tle	-nge

And here are complete words to match those endings:

abandon	flask
puppy	endings
hamper	Brandreth
breathe	market
maximum	messy
cattle	hinge

In the event of a tie, with two players declaring that they have completed their lists at the very same moment, the player whose list contains the longer words is declared the winner.

Alphabetic Narrative

Within a time limit of, say, ten minutes, each player has to compose a sentence, story or verse consisting of twenty-six words beginning with successive letters of the alphabet. The player whose effort is judged to be the best – the most logical or the most amusing – is the winner.

'X', as is often the case, is the stumbling block. Here is an example of one player's (mediocre) effort:

All bandsmen carry drums, every flautist guards his instrument jealously. Knowing lots more notes, orchestral players quickly rehearse symphonies. Try using violins with xylophones, you zealots!

Short Story

The players are given a set period of time, say fifteen minutes, in which to write a simple story using only words with four or fewer letters. At the end of the time limit, the players read out their stories and the player who has written the longest, most lucid and most entertaining story is the winner.

It sounds simple, but it isn't — especially when you remember that one five-letter word inadvertently used will mean that you are disqualified. Here is a brief Love Story to give you an idea of the game's scope — and its limitations.

It was in May a year or two ago that I met the fair Miss Anne Bun. She was just a slip of a girl and I was a man on the edge of ripe old age. We had tea on that cool May morn on the lawn at her Pa's seat near Deal by the sea. She was fun and full of life. I was grey and full of woe, but she did not seem to mind. I do not feel she fell in love with me just so that she and her vile Mama were able to have the vast sums of cash that I keep in a bank in town. She said that from the time she was a baby her wish had been to meet a man with a leg made of wood and with a red wig and that she was full of joy that at long last I had come to her. Yes, she said, to be my one and only wife was what she did want — and so did her Mama. (Her Papa was deaf and so had no say in the case, poor soul.) If I gave her all my cash she'd give me all her love. It was a fair deal and I was keen to say yes, but fate took a hand and said no, Miss Anne Bun is not to be your wife. She is to be run over by a big red bus on her way to the wee kirk on the hill. And that is what came to pass, alas, so that is the end of my sad tale. Take pity on me and weep for me as I lie all on my own in my old man's bed with only the idea of my lost love by me.

Short Short Story

If you thought the previous game was too easy, then this game should appeal to you. The rules are the same as before, except that no word used may contain more than *three* letters.

Here is an example of the sort of story that could be produced:

> A man had a pig in a sty. He fed it day by day. It ate all he fed it. But one day the pig bit the man on the leg. By gum, the man was mad! Now the pig is ham in a can.

(And if you think this is too easy, I'll leave you to write a story in which no word contains more than two letters!)

Stepping Stones

This is a mentally stimulating game of word associations, which may be played on any level from the banal to the esoteric. Each player in turn is given five themes by the other players. For example, a player may be told to get from 'Music' to 'Astronomy' via 'Cookery', 'Finance' and 'Auto-mobiles'. He may use up to nine statements or phrases and must touch on each of the themes in the order given. The other players, acting collectively as umpires, must satisfy themselves that all the themes have been touched on, that the sequence of associations is valid, and that any puns, allusions and the like are not too far-fetched.

Here are two ways in which the example quoted might work out in practice:

1. A note may be flat or sharp. (*Music*)
2. Knives used in the kitchen should always be sharp. (*Cookery*)
3. Knives are used for cutting.
4. The government will soon cut interest rates. (*Finance*)
5. We can then afford to borrow more.
6. I first learned to drive in a Ford. (*Automobiles*)
7. I now drive a Rolls.
8. The Rolling Stones are rock stars.
9. Stars, in fact, are formed from gas not from rock. (*Astronomy*)

1. Musicians usually begin by learning scales. (*Music*)
2. Scales are found on fish.
3. Salmon is the fish most often served with salads. (*Cookery*)
4. Salmon may be caught from river banks.

5. Banks are financial institutions. *(Finance)*
6. Automatic cash dispensers are used in many banks.
7. Automatic transmission makes driving easier. *(Automobiles)*
8. When driving I like to listen to the radio.
9. Radio-telescopes are used by astronomers. *(Astronomy)*

Semordnilap

Semordnilap is, of course, *palindromes* spelled backwards. A semordnilap is defined as a word which, when spelled backwards, forms another word.

For example:

Liar − Rail
Tide − Edit
Evil − Live
Bard − Drab

The game of SEMORDNILAP may be played in two ways.

In the first version, the players are given a set amount of time in which they have to list as many semordnilaps as they can. The winner is the player who produces the longest list in the time allowed.

In the second version a question-master gives the players clues to specific semordnilaps. For example: 'Reverse an eastern ruler to get frost' (answer: Emir & Rime), 'Reverse a beast to get a thin plate or layer' (answer: Animal & Lamina).

Word Ladders

In 1879 Lewis Carroll wrote a letter to *Vanity Fair* introducing a new kind of puzzle: 'The rules of the puzzle are simple enough. Two words are proposed of the same length; and the puzzle consists in linking these together by interposing other words, each of which shall differ from the next word *in one letter only*. That is to say, one letter may be changed in one of the given words, then one letter in the word so obtained, and so on, till we arrive at the other given word. The letters must not be interchanged among themselves, but each must keep to its own place. As an example, the word 'head' may be changed into 'tail' by interposing the words "heal, teal, tell tall".'

This now well-known puzzle forms the basis of an excellent game. Two related words with the same number of letters are chosen – *sleep*

and *dream*, *flour* and *bread*, *poor* and *rich*, *black* and *white*, *chin* and
nose – and the aim is to see which player can transform one word into the
other in the fewest steps.

For example, I have transformed *winter* into *summer* in nine steps –
perhaps you can do it in fewer.

                      W I N T E R
                      W I N D E R
                      W A N D E R
                      W A R D E R
                      H A R D E R
                      H A R P E R
                      H A M P E R
                      H A M M E R
                      H U M M E R
                      S U M M E R

Acrosticals

A word of six or seven letters is chosen, and each player writes the word
in a column on the left side of his sheet of paper. He then writes the same
word in another column some distance to the right of the first one, but
this time with the letters in reverse order. Let us say the chosen word is
Dreamer, then each player's sheet of paper should look something like
this:

            D   R
            R   E
            E   M
            A   A
            M   E
            E   R
            R   D

The players are then given a set time – five or ten minutes – in which
they have to write the longest word they can think of, beginning and
ending with each pair of letters provided by the two columns.

The players score one point per letter for each of their words, and the
player with the highest total score is the winner.

With this particular example, my best effort is shown below. Can
you beat my total score of 106?

DEMISEMIQUAVER	= 14
RECONNAISSANCE	= 14
ELECTROENCEPHALOGRAM	= 20
ABRACADABRA	= 11
MULTIMILLIONAIRE	= 16
ELECTRODYNAMOMETER	= 18
RECAPITULATED	= 13

Stairway

A letter of the alphabet is chosen (avoiding difficult letters like K, X or Z) and the players have a set time – ten minutes, say – in which to form a 'Stairway' of words beginning with that letter. The stairway consists of a two-letter word, then a three-letter word, then a four-letter word, and so on. Here is an example for the letter L:

L
LO
LOT
LONG
LEAST
LAGOON
LONGBOW
LIMERICK
LAMPSHADE
LOCOMOTION
LEGISLATION
LIFELESSNESS
LIBRARIANSHIP
LIBERTARIANISM

The winner is the player who forms the longest stairway within the set time.

Twisting Stairway

In the game of STAIRWAY the words forming the steps are not related to one another except in that they all begin with the same letter and are of increasing length. In TWISTING STAIRWAY, on the other hand, each step is formed by rearranging the letters of the previous step and adding one more letter. This makes it a somewhat more difficult game.

A letter is called out, and the players have a set time – about fifteen minutes would be appropriate – in which to attempt to build the longest twisting stairway they can.

For example, starting with the letter R:

R
RE
ARE
REAL
ALTER
RETAIL
RELIANT
ENTRAILS

Telegrams

A word of seven or more letters having been chosen, it is written down by each of the players. The players then have five minutes in which each of them has to compose a telegram, the words of which must begin with the letters of the chosen word in the correct order. For example, if the chosen word is *telegrams*, a player might produce:

TAKE EACH LETTER: EXPAND: GENERATE REALLY
APPROPRIATE MESSAGE SPEEDILY

The telegram need not necessarily be relevant to the chosen word, but if it is then so much the better.

When the five minutes is up, each player reads out what he has written, and the player whose telegram is judged to be the cleverest or most amusing is the winner.

Initials

Two words are chosen – any words will do, provided that they are both the same length and contain at least seven letters. Each player writes the words in two vertical columns, side by side, on the left side of his sheet of paper.

Say, for example, the words chosen were *weeping* and *spanner*.

Each player's sheet of paper should look something like this:

```
W  S
E  P
E  A
P  N
I  N
N  E
G  R
```

The object of the game is to use these letters as sets of initials, and to think of the name of a famous person (living or dead) to fit each set of initials. The first player to complete his list of names matching the initials is the winner.

In this particular example, one possible solution would be as follows:

```
W  S  – William Shakespeare (poet)
E  P  – Elvis Presley (singer)
E  A  – Edward Albee (dramatist)
P  N  – Paul Newman (film star)
I  N  – Isaac Newton (scientist)
N  E  – Nelson Eddy (actor-singer)
G  R  – George Robey (music-hall comedian)
```

Convergence

CONVERGENCE is a very entertaining game for two players in which each player thinks of a four-word sentence which his opponent has to guess.

Each player writes down a four-word sentence without letting the other player see what it is – the only restriction is that the sentence must not contain any proper nouns. Then player 1 makes his first guess at the other player's mystery sentence by calling out a test sentence. Player 2 tells him how near his guess was by saying, for each of the four words in the test sentence, whether the corresponding word in the mystery sentence is before or after it in alphabetical or dictionary sequence. Player 2 then makes his guess at the first player's mystery word and is given similar information.

Play continues in this way, with each player guessing in turn, until one of them wins the game by correctly identifying his opponent's mystery sentence.

Here, as an example, is one player's first few guesses from a typical game, showing how quickly you can home in on your opponent's sentence:

Mystery sentence: RED ROSES LOOK PRETTY.

Guess 1: MY HAIR IS GREY. – After, After, After, After

Guess 2: TRAMS SEEM RATHER NOISY – Before, Before, Before, Before

> (1st. word is between MY & TRAMS)
> (2nd. word is between HAIR & SEEMS)
> (3rd. word is between IS & RATHER)
> (4th. word is after NOISY)

Guess 3: NEVER READ MAD ROMANCES – After, After, Before, Before

> (1st. word is between NEVER & TRAMS)
> (2nd. word is between READ & SEEMS)
> (3rd. word is between IS & MAD)
> (4th. word is between NOISY & ROMANCES)

Guess 4: POET'S RUN LIKE PANTHERS – After, Before, After, After

> (1st. word is between POETS & TRAMS)
> (2nd. word is between READ & RUN)
> (3rd. word is between LIKE & MAD)
> (4th. word is between PANTHERS & ROMANCES)

Guess 5: ROUGH ROBBERS LOVE QUICHE – Before, After, Before, Before

> (1st. word is between POETS & ROUGH)
> (2nd. word is between ROBBERS & RUN)
> (3rd. word is between LIKE & LOVE)
> (4th. word is between PANTHERS & QUICHE)

Guess 6: RAINBOW RUGS LOOK PLEASANT – After, Before, Correct, After

> (1st. word is between RAINBOW & RUGGED)
> (2nd. word is between ROBBERS & RUGS)
> (3rd. word is LOOK)
> (4th. word is between PLEASANT & QUICHE)

Orthographic Invigilation

First gather together a group of people who pride themselves on their vocabulary and spelling ability. Then tell them that you are about to conduct an orthographic invigilation. Of course, they will know that this is what lesser mortals call a spelling test.

What you do is dictate the following passage to them, and then check their transcriptions. A result of more than 25 errors is poor, 15 is average, 5 is exceptional, and anyone who transcribes it faultlessly must surely have cheated.

The infectious proclivity for polysyllabic interchange of incomprehensible and occasionally irrefutable and unanswerable ratiocination, invective and oftentimes laryngeal trivialities is a poltroonery that is permissible of the most censorious and punitive retaliation. To possess an aggrandized vocabulary is a mental endowment transcending the encyclopaedical attributes of pedadogues who must investigate, peruse, and burrow for the scintillating segments of verisimilitude normally secreted from those whose knowledge is enchorial and whose verbiage is enclitic.

Exuberant and exultant propensities in phraseology continually lead to cerebral extradition for malefactors guilty of philological pyrotechnics. Perspicacious pundits scrupulously shun irreverent behaviourism and invariably take innocent refuge in the incontestable sanctuary of benign blandiloquence. Or by way of antithetical alternative, in mundane myopia.

Malicious malingerers in the realm of obsequious vacuity intermittently and agonizingly bewail the punctiliousness of those superlatively heirloomed with the gifts of psychic penetration. To their pettifogging mentalities any laboriously contrived device so minutely registering a mechanism as a micro-motoscope would loom gargantuan by invidious comparison. To elucidate for the benefit of such individuals would parallel the espousal of eudaemonics by Italo-Ethiopian aesthetes. One unmitigated and undisputed contention is that philological parsimoniousness is particularly preferable to loquacious laxity, especially as demonstrated by evanescent nincompoops of the lower cerebral classification.

Grid Games

Alphabet Race

This is a pencil and paper game for two players in which they race to see who can use all twenty-six letters of the alphabet first.

Each player has a piece of paper on which he has written out the complete alphabet, and there is a third piece of paper which serves as the 'board'. The players take it in turn to write words on the board, making sure that the word they play attaches (crossword-fashion) at some point to a word already played. A player may use each letter only once, and when he has written it on the board he must cross it off his list. For example, if the opening player begins by writing OPEN on the board, he then crosses the letters O, P, E and N off his list. His opponent must now write a word that he can attach to OPEN, for example ZOO:

```
          Z
          O
          O P E N
```

He now crosses the letters Z and O off his list, because they are the two letters he has played.

The first player to use all twenty-six of his letters wins the game. If a stage is reached when neither player can play, the player who has used most of his letters at that point is the winner. The words themselves do not score points: the sole aim of the game is to be the first one to use up the alphabet.

Here is how the board might look at the end of a game. The first player's words are written in capitals. His opponent's words are in lower-case letters.

```
        d                 W
      f u r                I
        m         c a b l  e
        p         h     L     Z
        S C Y T H E     D o z i n g
                  s         x   p
                  t
        Y O U N G
                  R
                W A X
                  B
```

When the stalemate was reached, the player using capitals still had five letters unused and the player using lower-case letters had only four, thus becoming the winner.

Trackword

Choose a nine-letter word, perhaps by opening a book at random and taking the first nine-letter word that appears. Then write the chosen word in a three-by-three grid. If, for example, the chosen word was Elephants, it would appear thus:

E	L	E
P	H	A
N	T	S

Each of the players then has to compile a list of as many words as he can, of at least three letters, from the word in the grid. Words are formed by tracking from letter to letter, up, down, across or diagonally. In this example, a player's list could include the following words:

lea	heal
least	hale
east	eat
ale	shale
stale	sale
last	plea
lathe	pleat

A time-limit, say ten minutes, should be set up. At the end of that time, the player with the most words on his list is the winner.

Crossword

To prepare for the game a square grid is drawn with nine squares across and nine squares down. A larger grid may be used if a longer game is required.

The first player writes a word anywhere in the grid, either across or down, scoring one point for each letter used. The players then play alternately, each player forming another word which must interlock with one or more of the words already entered in the grid, scoring 1 point for each letter added. For example if a player writes in the word ANAGRAM, intersecting with the G and M or previously entered words, he scores 5 points – he cannot claim points for the G and M already entered.

Play continues until neither player can find further letters that can be inserted to form new words. The player with the highest score is the winner.

Five By Five

This is a game for two players. Each player draws a grid five squares wide and five deep. The players do not let each other see their own grids until the game is over.

The two players take it in turns to call out letters. When a player calls out a letter he puts it into one of the squares on his grid. His opponent must also put the called-out letter somewhere on his grid. This continues until twenty-five letters have been called out, when the two grids will be full.

The object of the game is to fill your own grid with three-, four- and five-letter words going horizontally and vertically. At the end of the game you score 3 points for every three-letter word, 4 for every four-letter word, and 5 for every five-letter word.

Of course, the letters you call out will be ones designed to help you make words in your grid. Your opponent will have to accommodate the letters you call out in his grid as best he can. When he calls out his letters they will be ones he thinks will help him make words for his grid and you will then have to try to make the most of the letters he gives you.

Here is what the two grids looked like at the end of a game between Adam and Eve, in which Adam called out the letters R, G, E, L, A, S, O, L, I, P, E, L and S, and Eve called out A, N, C, H, O, R, E, A, E, N, D, and V.

R A N C H	G R A P E
O G R E A	R O E L A
P E E L S	O L V I C
E N D L V	A L E E H
S O L I A	N S N D S
Adam's grid	Eve's grid

Here is what each player scored:
ADAM: Words across – RANCH (5), OGRE (4), PEELS (5), END (3); Words down – ROPES (5), AGE (3), RED (3), CELL (4), HAS (3). Total: 35 points

EVE: Words across – GRAPE (5), ROE (3), ALE (3);
Words down – GROAN (5), ROLLS (5), EVEN (4), PLIED (5), EACH (4).
Total: 34 points.

One- and two-letter words do not count, and each letter can only be counted once in either direction. For example, in her top horizontal line Eve can only score for GRAPE, she cannot also score for RAPE, RAP or APE.

To add an extra dimension to the game, a bonus of 10 points can be awarded to any player who manages to form a five-letter word running diagonally from the top left-hand corner of his grid to the bottom right-hand corner.

Scramble

Each player draws – or is supplied with – an empty grid consisting of ten squares across and ten squares down. A theme is then chosen – which should be a fairly general one, such as Music, Transport, Art, Science, Food or Sport.

What each player has to do is to fill in his grid with interlocking words, blanking out unused squares where appropriate, so as to form a crossword. All the words entered must have some relevance to the chosen theme.

A crossword is deemed to be complete when at least half the squares – 50 in the case of a 10 × 10 grid – have been filled with letters and the remaining squares blanked out. The first player to complete his crossword calls out 'Stop!'. The other players may then finish any word they happen to be writing at that time, but must not start entering any new words.

Each player then passes his crossword to the player on his left for checking. A word is only valid if it interlocks with others, is correctly spelled and is relevant to the theme. Words of doubtful relevance should be put to a vote. If all the words are valid, a player scores 1 point for each letter entered in the grid. In the case of an invalid word, no points are scored for its letters except for those that interlock with, and thus form part of, a valid word.

To avoid arguments, certain rules should be agreed before you start. For example, supposing the theme is Music:

(a) Do you allow proper names such as *Ravel*?
(b) Do you allow abbreviations such as *pp* (for pianissimo)?
(c) Do you allow the same word to be used twice in a crossword – or variations of the same word, e.g. *drum* and *drums*?

(d) Do you allow phrases such as *in tune?*

If you like, you can add the refinement that the player who stops the game gets an extra 10 points if his is the highest letter score but loses 10 points if any other player has a higher letter score.

Here is an example with Music as the theme.

Sinko

SINKO is a game for two players that sounds simple but is challenging and stimulating to play.

A 5 × 5 grid is drawn, and the first player enters a five-letter word in any one of the five rows or five columns. The second player then enters another five-letter word either parallel to the first or interlocking with it.

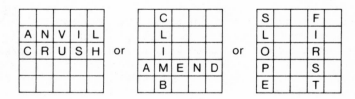

Then each player in turn enters another five-letter word, either horizontally or vertically. The game ends when a player is unable to fill in another word, either because the grid is full, or because he cannot find a word that will fit in with any of the letters previously entered.

Here, as an example, is the grid from a game in which the words played were as follows:

Player 1: PLAIN
Player 2: TAKEN
Player 1: MINOR
Player 2: SHEET
Player 1: VIDEO
Player 2: SPASM

S		T	V	
P	L	A	I	N
A		K	D	
S	H	E	E	T
M	I	N	O	R

Player 1 has lost because, understandably, he could not think of a word in the form S-TV-, A-KD-, -L-HI or -N-TR.

Letter Games

The Initial Letter Game

'Delightful, delicious, delectable, dainty Deborah Diamante, dare-devil Danny Diamante's dimpled daughter, demanded desperate decisions, despising diffident doubters.'

That is the intriguing opening of one player's effort in the INITIAL LETTER GAME, the aim of which is to write the longest story using words beginning all with the same letter.

You can play the game on your own, or you can give all the players pencil and paper and let them have ten minutes in which to concoct their stories. When the time is up, the player with the longest story that makes sense wins the game.

A, B, C, D, E, F, G, H, L, M, N, R, S, T and W are the letters to use. If you try playing with the other letters, the game is almost impossible.

Say It With Letters

How do you spell 'vacant' in two letters? Answer: MT. How do you spell 'disintegration' in two letters? Answer: DK.

SAY IT WITH LETTERS is a game in which the players have to identify 'words' like MT and DK (and IV and NRG and XLNC) and may be played in two ways.

In the first version the players are given clues as above, from which they have to guess the correct answers. The player getting the most correct answers is the winner.

The other way to play is to set the players the task of listing as many such 'words' as they can think of in a given amount of time. The winner is the player producing the longest list.

Jotto

JOTTO is a game of logical deduction for two players in which each player has to guess a mystery word chosen by the other.

Each.player writes down a five-letter word without letting the other player see what it is. Then each in turn calls out a five-letter word and the other player responds by saying how many letters of the test word correspond with letters in the word to be guessed.

For example:

Mystery word:	SLEEP
Guess 1:	THROW — no letters in common
Guess 2:	CREST — 2 letters
Guess 3:	STYLE — 3 letters

Play continues, with each player guessing alternately, until one or the other wins the game by correctly identifying his opponent's mystery word.

Here, as an example, are one player's guesses from a typical game, showing the sort of reasoning that is required:

1.	DANCE	1 letter	
2.	SANDY	2 letters	
3.	HANDY	1 letter	(So there must be an S and no H)
4.	SOUND	1 letter	(Eliminating O, U, N, D — from guess 2 there must be an A or Y)
5.	SUNNY	1 letter	(That eliminates Y. The word contains S, A — from guess 1, that eliminates C, E)
6.	FAILS	2 points	(Eliminating F, I, L)
7.	STRAP	4 letters	(The word must contain two of the letters of T, R, P)
8.	GRASP	3 letters	(So there's T and no G — we now have S, A, T plus either R or P and one other or a repeated letter)
9.	STAMP	3 letters	(So it's S, T, A and R and another — no M or P)
10.	STRAW	5 letters	— that's it!

Bulls And Cows

BULLS AND COWS is a variation of JOTTO. It is played in the same way except that each time a player calls out his test word he is told:
(a) how many letters of his test word correspond with letters in the mystery word in the same position (number of bulls);
(b) how many letters of his test word correspond with letters in the mystery word but in different positions (number of cows).

For example:

Mystery word:	TRAIN	
Guess 1:	ABOVE	1 cow
Guess 2:	PRINT	1 bull, 2 cows
Guess 3:	GRAND	2 bulls, 1 cow

Double Jeopardy

DOUBLE JEOPARDY is another variation of JOTTO, which was invented by Don Laycock, an Australian games designer. The rules are the same as for JOTTO, except that when a player calls out his test word he must at the same time declare how many letters of the test word correspond with letters in *his own* mystery word.

This means that test words need to be selected with great care – because you want to glean as much information as you can about your opponent's mystery word while at the same time revealing as little as possible about your own.

Crash

CRASH is yet another variation on the JOTTO theme, and in fact it could be described as BULLS AND COWS without the cows.

Rules are as for JOTTO, except that when a player calls out his test word he is told only the number of 'crashes' – that is, the number of matching letters in the same position in both the test word and the mystery word.

For example:

Mystery word:	STARE	
Guess 1:	ASTER	– no crashes
Guess 2:	STONE	– 3 crashes

Uncrash

A 'crash' may be defined as the situation in which two words of equal length have the same letter in the same position. For example, in the case of *stop* and *pest*, there is no crash – although they have letters in common, they do not occur in the same position in each word. In the case of *last* and *hose*, however, they both have the letter s in the third position – that is a 'crash'.

UNCRASH is a game for two to four players. Player 1 writes down a word of an agreed length, say three letters. The second player then writes underneath it another three-letter word that does not have any crashes with the previous word. The players then continue, in turn, each placing at the end of the list a new word that has no crashes with any of the previous words. This goes on until a player is unable to add a new word without causing a crash. That player loses the round and is eliminated. The remaining players continue to play further rounds until the winner has eliminated all his opponents.

Here is a sample game, in which player 2 lost because he could not think of a word to add after emu:

Player 1:	RUB
Player 2:	ASK
Player 3:	TRY
Player 1:	DIN
Player 2:	OLD
Player 3:	LET
Player 1:	WAR
Player 2:	HOG
Player 3:	BYE
Player 1:	EMU

Ten-Letter Challenge

A ten-letter word is chosen as a starter – preferably one that does not have many duplications of letters. *Orchestral, tambourine, aerobatics, diagnostic, balustrade, stimulated* and *hinterland*, for example, would all make suitable starter words. Each player writes the chosen starter word in a column down the left side of his sheet of paper.

A time limit is set – say, ten minutes – and in that time each player has to find the longest word he can starting with each letter of the starter word, but using only letters contained in the starter word itself. For the first letter of the starter word you may not use the starter itself or any word derived from the same root. That is, if the starter word is *orchestral*, for example, your word beginning with the letter O cannot be *orchestral* or *orchestra*. If a letter is duplicated in the starter word, you must have a different word for each occurrence of that letter.

When the time is up, the players score 1 point per letter in each of the words they have formed, and the player with the highest total is the winner.

Here is what one player achieved with *orchestral* as his starter word:

Others	= 6	Starch	= 6
Reacts	= 6	Torches	= 7
Chortles	= 8	Reach	= 5
Harlots	= 7	Arches	= 6
Earths	= 6	Lathers	= 7

Total 64

Centurion

The game of CENTURION was invented by David Parlett and is an excellent two-player game for those adept with numbers as well as with words.

The letters from A to Z are assigned numerical values according to their position in the alphabet.

A	1		N	14
B	2		O	15
C	3		P	16
D	4		Q	17
E	5		R	18
F	6		S	19
G	7		T	20
H	8		U	21
I	9		V	22
J	10		W	23
K	11		X	24
L	12		Y	25
M	13		Z	26

Player 1 starts off by writing down any three-letter word which has a total value of 10 or less – which tends to mean the choice is between *ace*, *add*, *aga*, *aha*, *bad*, *bag*, *cab*, *cad*, *dab*, *dad*, and *fad* – and writes the values of the word beside it.

Player 2 then writes under the first word another three-letter word which must start with the last letter of the first word. Beside that he writes the value of the word and the cumulative total.

For example:

ADD	9
DIE	18 + 9 = 27

The players then continue, in turn, adding another three-letter word that starts with the final letter of the previous word, keeping count of the cumulative value. The first player to make the total go over 99 is the loser.

ADD	9
DIE	18 + 9 = 27
EEL	22 + 27 = 51
LOP	43 + 51 = 94

Since the lowest-scoring word that can be used to continue is PAD, scoring 21, Player 1 loses in this sample game.

Double Centurion

DOUBLE CENTURION is a variation of CENTURION that may be played by up to four players. Rules are the same as for the previous game except that it is the player making the total reach 200 who loses.

Letter Nim

NIM is an old-fashioned game in which two players alternately take a number of objects from a pile, the winner being either the player who takes the last object or the player who forces his opponent to do so. LETTER NIM is a tactical word game for two players, based on the same principle.

The alphabet is written out from A to Z. The first player then writes down a word beginning with A, and A is crossed off the alphabet to show it has been used. If the word contains a B, that letter is also crossed off. If the word contains a C following the B, C is crossed off. The same applies to a D following the C, and so on.

Thus *anchor* would delete only the A; *album* would cause the A and B to be deleted; *ambulance* the A, B and C; *abscond* the A, B, C and D; *absconder* the A, B, C, D and E.

The next player then writes a word beginning with the first letter in the alphabet that has not yet been crossed off. As before, he crosses off that letter and any consecutive letters of the alphabet after that which appear in the correct sequence in his word.

Here is a sample game:

Player 1:	ABACUS	(deleting A, B, C)
Player 2:	DEFENDING	(deleting D, E, F, G)
Player 1:	HIJACK	(deleting H, I, J, K)
Player 2:	LEMON	(deleting L, M, N)
Player 1:	OPAQUE	(deleting O, P, Q)
Player 2:	REST	(deleting R, S, T)
Player 1:	UNDER	(deleting U)
Player 2:	VOW	(deleting V, W)
Player 1:	XYLOPHONE	(deleting X, Y)
Player 2:	ZAP	(deleting Z)

You can decide which way you prefer to play the game – whether the player using the Z is the winner or the loser. It is preferable, however, if both players come to the same decision!

Word Ping-Pong

This two-player game was invented by P. Perkins and first published in *Games and Puzzles* magazine. The basic idea of the game is the same as that of WORD LADDERS (see page 45) – that is, a list of words is formed by changing one letter at a time to form a new word. I have altered the original rules of this game somewhat, and I think the result is a very enjoyable game.

The first player 'serves' by writing down a four-letter word, in which the letters are all different. Then each player in turn alters one letter to form a new word which is written underneath the previous word. The first player may change only the first or second letter, and the second player may change only the third or fourth letter. In each turn the letter that is changed must be changed to a completely new letter – one that has not appeared anywhere in any of the previous words.

A valid 'serve' must give the second player a chance to respond – that is, it must consist of a word that is capable of having its third or fourth letter changed to form a new word. So serving *cyan* or *cwms*, for example, would be a fault, and one point would go to the opposite player. Also, the same word may not be served more than once in a game.

A player loses when he is unable to form a new word in accordance with the rules.

Here is a sample rally:

LONG	(Player 1 serves)
LONE	(Player 2 – new letter E)
LINE	(Player 1 – new letter I)
LINK	(Player 2 – new letter K)
MINK	(Player 1 – new letter M)
MINT	(Player 2 – new letter T)
HINT	(Player 1 – new letter H)
HIND	(Player 2 – new letter D)
HAND	(Player 1 – new letter A)
HARD	(Player 2 – new letter R)
CARD	(Player 1 – new letter C)
CARP	(Player 2 – new letter P)
WARP	(Player 1 – new letter W)
WASP	(Player 2 – new letter S)

Player 1 loses because he cannot follow on from *wasp*. I, G, H and R have already appeared in previous words, so he cannot play *wisp*, *gasp*, *hasp* or *rasp*.

In keeping with the name of the game, you can use the scoring system of Ping-Pong (otherwise known as Table Tennis). A rally is a round of play starting with a service and ending with one player scoring a point. Each player serves (goes first) for five successive rallies, and then there is a change of service. The winner is the first player to score 21 points, except that if the score reaches 20–20, service alternates with each rally and the winner has to establish a 2-point lead over his opponent.

Verbal Sprouts

To start, a four-letter word is formed by each player in turn writing a circled letter in a horizontal line. The letters must be all different and must form a word. The circled letters are then joined by arrows, like this:

$$(H) \rightarrow (A) \rightarrow (R) \rightarrow (E)$$

Then each player in turn adds a new circled letter to the diagram and connects it with arrows to one or more existing letters to form further words. The letter added must be different from any letters already entered in the diagram. The player then scores one point per letter for each word he can make, using his newly entered letter and following the arrows in the diagram.

For example, from the starting position shown above, the first player could insert the letter T and add the appropriate arrows to form the words *hart*, *hate*, *tear* and *earth*, scoring 17 points.

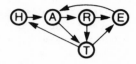

The second player might then add the letter D to the diagram.

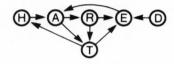

This enables him to make the words Dearth and Death, giving him 11 points.

The game continues in this way until neither player is able to add a new letter to form further words. The player with the highest score is then the winner.

There are a few additional rules to bear in mind:

(a) Arrows may not cross one another.
(b) There can never be more than one arrow between any given pair of letters. Thus, in our example, where there is an arrow from A to R, you could not add an arrow going from R to A.
(c) Words may only be made by following the direction of the arrows.
(d) No letter may have more than four arrows attached to it (whether leading to or from the letter). Thus, in our example, T has its full complement of arrows after it has been connected to the H.
(e) Points may not be scored for words entirely contained within a longer word. So the player scoring 6 points for Dearth, for example, could not also claim 4 points for Dear.

Collection Games

Categories

The players decide on a list of categories – preferably about twenty. The fairest way to choose them is to let each player propose an equal number of categories.

Each player writes down the list of categories on his sheet of paper, and then a letter of the alphabet is chosen at random. A time limit is agreed – ten minutes, let us say. The players then have to write down as many words as they can that begin with the chosen letter for each of the categories.

When the time is up, each player passes his list to the person on his left for checking. The words listed for each category are read out. A word which has not been thought of by any other player scores 2 points; a word which one or more other players have also listed scores only 1 point. The player with the highest total is the winner.

For subsequent rounds a new initial letter is chosen.

Guggenheim

A list of categories is chosen and each player writes the list down the left-hand side of his sheet of paper. A keyword of five or more letters, all different, is then chosen, and each player writes the keyword, well spaced out, along the top of his sheet of paper.

A time limit is set, and each player must then attempt to write down one word beginning with each letter of the keyword for each category.

For example, with a keyword of Track, one player's list might look something like this:

	T	**R**	**A**	**C**	**K**
Countries	Turkey	Russia	Austria	Canada	Kenya
Birds	Turkey	Raven	Auk	Coot	Kite
Rivers	Thames	Rhine	Aire	Coquet	Kennet
Novelists	Trollope	Roth	Asimov	Conrad	Kafka
Weapons	Torpedo	Rifle	Assegai	Club	Kris
Boats	Trawler	Raft	Ark	Canoe	Ketch
Drinks	Tea	Retsina	Ale	Cider	Kummel
Flowers	Thistle	Rose	Aster	Camellia	Kingcup

Animal Magic

Equip all the players with pencil and paper and give them ten minutes in which to write down all the adjectives they can think of that have their origin in birds and beasts but which, as adjectives, may be applied to human beings. Here are some examples:

Asinine	Foxy
Bitchy	Lousy
Bovine	Mulish
Catty	Ratty
Dogged	Sheepish
Elephantine	Sluggish
Fishy	Swinish

When the time is up the player with the longest list of adjectives wins the game.

Since, curiously, so many of the adjectives refer to what are generally regarded as unpleasant or unattractive characteristics, any player who manages to include adjectives that have a pleasant connotation (Kittenish, for example) will be allowed 2 points for that one adjective.

Build-Up

The players are given a simple word onto which they must build up as many other words as they can think of. For example, if the given word is Head here are just some of the words that can be built up from it: headhunter, head-over-heels, headstrong, headlong, headquarters, headdress, headline, heading, heady, headache, headfast, header, headmost, headsman, headband, headgear.

If the players are given a set time-limit, say five or ten minutes, the player with the longest list when the time is up is the winner of the game.

To give the players even greater scope, as well as starting with short words that can be built up into longer ones, it is possible to start with prefixes. Here, for example, is a very small selection of the words you can build up from EX: exacerbate, exact, exactly, exaggerate, exalt, examine, example, exasperate, excavate, exceed, excel, except, exhibit, exhilarate, exhort, exigence, exiguous, exile, exist, exit, exorbitant, exotic, expand, expatiate.

Consecutives

The players, each armed with pencil and paper, have to list as many words as they can which contain two consecutive letters of the alphabet. A time-limit of, say, ten minutes is set for the performance of this task.

Among the words that might be listed are:

ABOUT	TUNE
DETAIL	OXYGEN
EFFORT	HYMN
GHOST	OPPOSITE

Scoring may be based on the total number of words listed or, alternatively, the number of *different* consecutive letter pairs in a player's list.

A variant of this game involves listing words which contain *three* consecutive letters of the alphabet, for example:

DABCHICK	FIRST
DEFY	STUDY
PLOUGHING	AFGHAN

This game, in either variation, is also suitable as an entertaining solo pastime.

Personal Words

Within the given time-limit, the players have to compile a list of words which are not only boys' or girls' names but are also common nouns that may be found in the dictionary without a capital initial letter.

Some examples are:

Lee	— the sheltered side
Lance	— a cavalry weapon
Warren	— a maze of narrow passages
Gene	— a unit of DNA
Ruth	— pity, sorrow
Carol	— a song

You should decide before starting the game whether or not you are going to allow the many girls' names that are also names of flowers or trees — Daisy, Violet, Rose, Olive, Hazel etc.

The player with the longest list is the winner.

Palindromic Words

Palindromic words are words that read the same when written backwards: Gag, Deed, Kayak etc.

Within a given time limit see which of the players can form the longest list of such words.

(Can you find a longer palindromic word than my nine-letter word Malayalam (an Asian language)?)

Animal Words

The objective of this game is to see who can form the longest list of words, each word to contain within it the name of an animal. Only one word per animal is allowed.

Some words that may be listed are: Kayak; Benevolent; Catch; Drapery; Foxglove.

Irregular Plurals

The aim is to see who can form the longest list of words which, in their plural form, do not end with the letter S.

Some typical examples are:

> Die / Dice
> Stigma / Stigmata
> Cherub / Cherubim
> Lied / Lieder

Before playing this game you should decide whether or not to allow words that are the same in the singular and plural — Fish, Sheep, etc.

Alpha

In this game each player is given a time-limit — ten minutes, say — in which to write down a list of words that begin and end with the same letter of the alphabet. Here are some examples: Clinic, Evade, Gag, Hash, Mum, Rider, Stress, Yesterday, and, of course, Alpha.

Naturally, you increase the potential number of words if you allow proper names (Cadillac, Xerox), foreign words (Uhuru), colloquialisms (zizz) and exclamations (Aha!, Wow!).

There are two different versions of the game.

In the first version, the players just list as many acceptable words as they can and, at the end of the set time, the player with the longest list is the winner.

In the second version, which is a more demanding test of vocabulary, each player first writes the letters of the alphabet down the left-hand margin of his piece of paper. Then for each letter he has to find the longest word which begins and ends with that letter. When the time-limit has expired, the players score 1 point for each letter of each word they have listed and the winner is the player with the highest total score. Thus Minimum (7 points) is preferable to Maim (4 points), and Metamorphism (12 points) is preferable to both.

Arena

The players are given a time-limit in which to form as long a list as possible of five-letter words which have vowels as their first, third and fifth letters, and consonants as their second and fourth letters.

Such a list might include the following words:

Arena	Opera	Unite
Aroma	Abide	Amuse
Evade	Image	Okapi

The player who produces the longest list is the winner.

Vowels

A particular vowel is chosen, and the players are given a set time in which to produce a list of words which must contain the given vowel at least twice and must contain no other vowels.

For example, if A is the chosen vowel, the following words would qualify: Ballad, Data, Atlas, Salad, Ballast, Anagram, Catamaran.

Players score one point for each occurrence of the chosen vowel in their words – thus Data scores 2 points but Catamaran scores 4. The player with the highest number of points is the winner.

Six And Two Threes

The players are given a set amount of time in which to list as many six-letter words as they can which can be split in half to form separate three-letter words.

For example:

> Carpet − Car & Pet
> Carton − Car & Ton
> Season − Sea & Son
> Redraw − Red & Raw
> Catkin − Cat & Kin

The winner is the player with the longest list at the end of the time allowed.

Roman Numeral Words

What do the words below have in common?

> LID   MILD
> CIVIL   MIX

The answer is that they are all formed entirely from letters that are also Roman numerals: I, V, X, L, C, D, M.

In this game the players are allowed five minutes in which they have to list as many words of this type as they can. The player with the longest list at the end of the time allowed is the winner.

Combinations

For this game you need to prepare a list of ten or more two-letter or three-letter combinations which could occur within words. Such a list might contain letter combinations such as these:

> gn   ido
> tr   rew
> mf   ump
> hn   tic
> bl   rve
> rp

Each of the players writes down the list on his sheet of paper. A time-limit is set –of ten minutes, say – in which each player has to find as long a word as possible containing each letter combination in the list. The scoring is 1 point per letter for each word, and the player obtaining the highest total number of points is the winner.

Using the combinations shown as an example a good player might achieve a result like this, giving a total score of 147:

Indignation	= 11
Theatrically	= 12
Circumferences	= 14
Pyrotechnical	= 13
Incorrigibleness	=16
Anthropomorphism	= 16
Kaleidoscopes	= 13
Wherewithal	= 11
Presumptuousness	= 16
Statisticians	= 13
Surveillance	= 12

Sequentials

A fixed time is set – say, ten minutes – in which each player has to list as many words as he can that contain two consecutive letters that are consecutive in the alphabet.

For example: Alphabet; Child; Elm.

The player producing the longest list is the winner.

That version of the game is probably more suitable for younger players – most adults would find it too easy as there are so many suitable words – words containing de, no, st, tu, etc – that it could become merely a test of how fast one can write. A more demanding version is to list only words containing three consecutive letters of the alphabet, for example: Defy; Sighing; First.

Beheadings

No, BEHEADINGS is not a variation of HANGMAN – it is a completely different game.

The players are given a set time in which they have to list as many words as they can which have the property of forming another word when the initial letter is removed.

For example:

Blight	(may be beheaded to form Light)
Every	(may be beheaded to form Very)
Stone	(may be beheaded to form Tone)
Hand	(may be beheaded to form And)

When the time is up, the players add up the number of words they have found, and the player with the longest list is the winner.

Children's Games

Hangman

This is a classic paper-and-pencil game for two players. One player thinks of a word, preferably of six or more letters, and the other player has to discover the word by guessing individual letters.

The first player writes down a series of dashes to indicate the number of letters in the mystery word, thus: ————————. The second player then starts guessing the letters in the word, calling out one letter at a time. If the letter occurs anywhere in the word the first player writes that letter above the appropriate dash (or dashes) wherever the letter occurs. But for each letter called out that does *not* occur in the mystery word, the first player adds an extra bit to the drawing of a gallows. The player who is doing the guessing has eleven lives to lose, in that the gallows consists of eleven parts:

1. The base of the gallows
2. The upright of the gallows
3. The arm of the gallows
4. The support
5. The rope
6. The victim's head

7. The victim's body
8. The victim's right arm
9. The victim's left arm
10. The victim's right leg
11. The victim's left leg

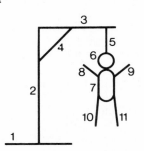

The incorrectly guessed letters are usually recorded underneath the gallows so that the second player can see which letters he has already tried.

If the gallows is completed before the second player has identified the word he is 'hanged' and loses, and the first player has another go at choosing a mystery word.

The second player wins if he correctly identifies the word before the gallows is completed. He then chooses a word for the other player to guess.

Sometimes the game is played using agreed themes, such as Book Titles or Names of TV Programmes, in which case the name or title to be guessed may consist of more than one word. In this case the first player will draw the dashes to show the number of letters in each word with spaces between the words.

Consequences

CONSEQUENCES is a classic word game that has been played around the world for generations and yet still manages to retain its peculiar charm. To play it, equip everyone with a pencil and a long sheet of paper. Then tell the players to write down certain pieces of information, and each time they have done so get them to fold the top of their pieces of paper forward (so as to conceal what they have written) and pass the paper to the player sitting on their right. Gradually the pieces of information build up into a story, and at the end of the game all the different stories are read out and the wittiest is given the warmest applause.

Traditionally a dozen pieces of information are called for, but you may amend these or add your own should you feel so inclined:

1. An adjective *(fold and pass)*
2. A girl's name *(fold and pass)*
3. The word MET plus and adjective *(fold and pass)*
4. A man's name *(fold and pass)*
5. The word AT plus details of where they met *(fold and pass)*
6. When they met *(fold and pass)*
7. The words HE SAID TO HER followed by what he said *(fold and pass)*
8. The words SHE SAID TO HIM followed by what she said *(fold and pass)*
9. What he then did *(fold and pass)*
10. What she then did *(fold and pass)*
11. The words AND THE CONSEQUENCE WAS plus details of the consequence *(fold and pass)*
12. The words AND THE WORLD SAID plus details of what the world did say.

First Names First

Each player is given a sheet of paper and a pencil, and a boy's or girl's name is called out. This should be a name of six or more letters, like Roland, for example.

Each player writes the letters of this name, well spaced out, across the top of his sheet of paper, and then has to list under each letter as many names as he can think of that begin with that letter. A time-limit is set, and when the time is up the player with the longest list of names is the winner.

In the case of Roland, a typical list might start like this:

R	O	L	A	N	D
Roland	Oliver	Luther	Anne	Neil	Dawn
Richard	Olive	Lucy	Abe	Natalie	Denis
Rachel	Oscar	Lesley	Andrew	Nicholas	David
Ruth		Laura	Arthur	Norma	Don
Rhoda			Alice	Norman	Daisy
Ralph			Amy	Nancy	Dwight
Rebecca					

Mirror Writing

Each player has his own sheet of paper and a pencil. The question-master reads out a sentence, and each player has to write that sentence in mirror writing. That is, when the paper is held up in front of a mirror, the writing reflected in the mirror has to appear the normal way round. It is surprising how difficult it can be to do this perfectly without a lot of practice.

The results are checked with the aid of an actual mirror, and the player whose effort is judged the best is declared to be the winner.

Sounds The Same

This game is based on homonyms – pairs of words that sound the same but are different in spelling and meaning: *throne* and *thrown*, *herd* and *heard*, *bough* and *bow*, for example.

The question-master reads out a list of such words, and the players have to write down the two different spellings for each word. The winner is the player who manages to write down the largest number of correct pears. I'm sorry, I mean pairs.

Other suitable pairs of words are:

Coarse & course	Links & lynx
Assent & ascent	Suede & swayed
Foul & fowl	Baize & bays
Allowed & aloud	Lax & lacks
Bold & bowled	Ball & bawl
Cereal & serial	Packed & pact
Clause & claws	Quarts & quartz
Colonel & kernel	Bolder & boulder
Council & counsel	Altar & alter
Signet & cygnet	Grown & groan
Muscle & mussel	Side & sighed
Pray & prey	Their & there
Soared & sword	Waist & waste
Pole & poll	Wood & would
Medal & meddle	Plain & plane

Synonyms

This game is an entertaining way of getting children to extend their vocabularies. A list of twenty words is read out, which the players must copy down on the left-hand side of their sheet of paper. The players are then given a time-limit in which they have to write down synonyms (words with the same meaning) for each of the given words. Some words may have more than one acceptable synonym, in which case the players may list as many as they like. When the time is up, the player with the longest and most accurate list of synonyms is the winner.

A suitable list of words for this game might include some of these:

Abide	Convey	Jump	Sailor
Adorn	Deadly	Keep	Sundry
Afraid	Educate	Lie	Tear
Aid	Error	Mild	Throw
Allow	Fall	Near	Under
Bad	Forbid	Observe	Vanish
Beat	Gift	Pull	Victory
Branch	Haste	Quiet	Wander
Careful	Huge	Rescue	Yokel
Choose	Idle	Rogue	Zero

Partners

This game requires a little preparation on the part of the question-master. He has to prepare a list of well-known pairs of partners. Suitable pairs might include:

Jack & Jill	Starsky & Hutch
Adam & Eve	Antony & Cleopatra
Tom & Jerry	Bonnie & Clyde
Laurel & Hardy	Abbott & Costello
Romeo & Juliet	The Owl & The Pussycat

The list might be extended to include phrases such as sugar and spice, bat and ball, stars and stripes, etc.

To play the game each player is given a sheet of paper and a pencil. The question-master reads out the first name of each pair, allowing a few seconds before moving on to the next pair. The players have to try to write down the name of the missing partner for each name read out. The player who correctly lists the most partners is the winner.

Nation Game

This game may be played in two ways. The players can either list as many words as they can that end with 'nation' or they can be given clues that lead them to the answers.

In the first version the players should be given a set amount of time to list words like: Designation, Donation, Examination, Imagination. The player who produces the longest list of words is the winner.

To play the game in the second way, the players need to be given clues to point them towards the 'nation' words. For example, 'Which nation is a flower?' (answer: Carnation), or 'Which nation sleeps through the winter?' (answer: Hibernation). Again the winner is the player with the longest list of correct answers at the end of the time allowed.

Ship Game

Like the NATION GAME, this game may be played in two ways.

The players may be given a set amount of time in which to list as many words as they can that end with ship – words like: Worship, Friendship, Ownership, Partnership, Scholarship. The player who produces the longest list of words is the winner.

Alternatively, the players may be given clues to point them to the 'ship' words. For example: 'Which ship commands others?' (answer: Leadership), or 'Which ship is shared by somebody else?' (answer: Partnership). Again the winner is the player with the longest list of correct answers at the end of the time allowed.

Jumbled Proverbs

Give each player a sheet of paper and a pencil and then read a list of proverbs to them. In every case the proverb has been jumbled, and the players have to unjumble the words and put them into the right order before writing down the proverb as it should read. These are some examples of proverbs you might include:

> Shines hay while the make sun.
>
> A silver has every lining cloud.
>
> The bush worth is a hand in bird two the in.

Children, especially those who may not know the proverbs well, will enjoy puzzling over ten to fifteen of these, trying to unscramble them. The player with the most correct answers wins.

Licence-Plate Words

This is an ideal game for keeping children amused on long car journeys. Tell them to keep their eyes open for complete words on the licence-plates of vehicles they see. For example:

CAT	MAT
MUM	FOR
LET	BAR
TOP	TON

A list should be kept of the words seen. The player with the longest list at the end of the journey is the winner.

Solo Games

Starting Point

You begin by writing any word of your choice on the middle of a blank piece of paper. Then give yourself ten minutes in which to build up a series of other words based on the starting word. The words must not only be physically linked to one another, they must also be broadly related to the theme set by the starting word. Here is an example in which the starting word is Entertainment:

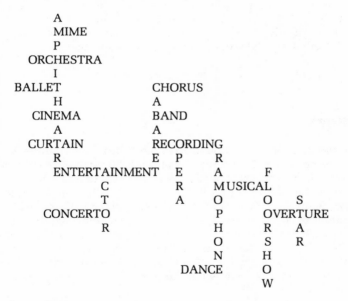

Twenty words in ten minutes isn't bad going, but the ease or difficulty of the game depends largely on the word you start with. Holidays, Animals, Pastimes and Education are easy starting words: Taxidermist, Follicle and Battery aren't. If you want to cheat, you can always start with the word Dictionary, in which case every word you choose to add could be said to be in some way linked to it!

One Hundred Word Challenge

Could you write a hundred words that make sense and not repeat a single word once? If you can, then you have mastered the game already because that's all it involves. Here is how Mrs Pearl Feldman and her pupils managed at Pompton Lakes High School, New Jersey, where the game originated:

> 'Let's go! The challenge is to write a composition without using any word more than once. Do you think that it can be done? If not, give one reason for doing this. While we are sitting here in English class at Pompton Lakes High School, Lakeside Avenue, New Jersey, all of us figure out something which makes sense. Mrs Feldman helps her pupils because another teacher said they couldn't accomplish such tasks. Nobody has fresh ideas right now. Goal – 100! How far did students get? Eighty-five done already; fifteen left. 'Pretty soon none!' says Dennis O'Neill. Gary Putnam and Debra Petsu agree. So there!'

If you think you can do better (and you probably can) have a go.

Network

First choose a category – Countries of the World, Towns, Birds, Rivers, Artists or whatever. Then form a list of words fitting the chosen category – the list may be as short or as long as you care to make it.

Now you have to fit your list of words into a diagram similar to that shown below. Each letter is written within a circle and the circled letters are connected by lines, horizontally, vertically or diagonally to form the words. (Diagonal lines are not, however, allowed to cross one another.)

The aim is to make as many as possible of the letters serve in more than one word, or, to put it another way, to make the diagram contain the maximum number of words but the minimum number of letters and connecting lines.

One suggested method of scoring is to score 10 points for each word in the network, minus 2 points for each letter used and minus 1 point for each connecting line.

So this simple example would score 8 points:

> 3 words (PEAR, PEACH, GRAPE) = 30 points
> 7 letters = − 14 points
> 8 connectors = − 8 points

Here is a more advanced example, scoring 27 points. See if you can work out for yourself how that score is reached.

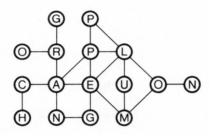

Safari For Literati

See how many names for species of mammal you can find that end with the letter I. (There are more than you probably think there are!)

My personal list includes seventeen species (not counting Yeti) ranging from Agouti − a South American rodent − to Wistiti (a type of marmoset). Can you do better than that?

Wordbuilder

To play this game all you have to do is take a word − any word will do, but preferably one of medium length − and form a list of as many other words as you can think of that may be formed from the letters in the given word. For example, if the starter word was Accidental, the following are some of the words that may be formed:

Acid	Cant	Dale	Tale
Aide	Candle	Date	Talc
Antic	Clan	Data	Tidal
Accident	Clad	Dace	Tide
Accent	Cent	Dental	Teal
Alien	Clean	Diet	Tail

The following rules are usually applied (but of course, you may modify the rules as you wish):

(a) Each word must contain at least four letters.
(b) Proper nouns are not allowed.
(c) Foreign words, abbreviations and plurals are not allowed.
(d) A letter may be used in any word no more than the number of times it occurs in the starter word.

Some other suitable starter words are:

Reasonable	Youngster	Tolerance
Avoidance	Brightness	Candlewick
Formidable	Centigrade	Remainder
Petroleum	Population	Orchestra
Promenade	Newspaper	Headstrong
Manifesto	Disastrous	Introduce

To play the game as a solo game, just choose your word and start scribbling. To play it as a game for two or more, give everyone the same word and the same amount of time, and see which player manages to come up with the longest list of acceptable words.

Category Crosswords

For this game you need a blank crossword grid. You can draw your own but it is much easier to cut out a crossword grid from a newspaper or magazine. Now choose a category – Countries, Birds, Book titles, Animals, Rivers, Artists, or whatever you like.

The aim of the game is to fill in the crossword grid, using only words connected with your chosen category. Entering the first few words is easy enough, but the task becomes progressively harder as you have to put in words that will connect with the letters of the words you have already entered. You will probably find that you often have to backtrack, and therefore a pencil (and eraser) will be found to be more suitable than a pen.

Half The Alphabet

What do the following words all have in common?

Called	Climbed
Ballad	Milkmaid
Alibi	Defiled
Deface	Gamble

The answer is that they use only letters from the first half of the alphabet — a to m. See how many words you can find that have the same property. What is the longest such word you can discover?

When you have done that you might like to consider words that use only letters from the second half of the alphabet.

Typewriter Words

The top row of letters on a standard typewriter keyboard consists of Q, W, E, R, T, Y, U, I, O, P. How many words can you find that contain only these letters? What is the longest such word you can find?

Here are a few words to start you off:

Pert	Pour
Pretty	Totter
Quip	Poetry
Quite	Tripper

The letters on the second row of the typewriter are: A, S, D, F, G, H, J, K, L. I shouldn't think there are so many words to be found using only these letters, as only one vowel is included. But have a go and see how many you can discover.

On the third row we have: Z, X, C, V, B, N, M. I think we can forget about finding words that use only these letters!

Theme Songs

Set yourself the task of seeing how many song titles you can think of to fit a given theme. Here are some examples, but you can, no doubt, make up many more of your own.

Song titles including the name of a country: *America*, *From Russia With Love*, *Slow Boat To China*, etc.

Song titles including a colour: *White Christmas*, *Yellow Submarine*, *Green Grow The Rushes-O*, etc. (If you want to make it more difficult you can restrict the theme to one particular colour such as red, green, white or blue.)

Song titles including or consisting of a girl's name: *Laura*, *Lucy In The Sky With Diamonds*, *Eleanor Rigby*, etc.

Song titles including a number: *Tea For Two*, *Three Coins In The Fountain*, *Ten Green Bottles*, etc.

Song titles including the name of a town or city: *Chicago*, *I Left My Heart In San Francisco*, *April In Paris*, etc.

This game may also be played with the titles of books or films if your tastes are literary or cinematic rather than musical.

Newspaper Headline Search Game

The language of newspaper headlines is quite different from English.

The vocabulary is different. There are no articles, definite or in-definite. In headlines people don't criticize or condemn, they rap or slam – 'Industry Boss Raps Unions', 'Reagan Slams Soviets'. They don't investigate, they probe – 'Police Probe Jewel Theft'.

The tenses are different too. For actions in the past, the present tense is used – 'Boy Saves Drowning Man'. And for actions in the future the infinitive is used – 'Film Star To Quit'.

But the aspect of headlines that appeals to me most is the noun-cluster. In my newspaper today there is the headline 'Gang Boss Trial Verdict'. Doubtless, I will soon be reading 'Gang Boss Trial Verdict Appeal' or even 'Gang Boss Trial Verdict Appeal Shock'. I might even see 'Gang Boss Trial Jury Corruption Probe Sensation'.

It is an amusing game to collect actual examples from your daily newspaper. What is the longest noun-cluster you can find? What is the funniest?

I haven't yet seen the headline 'Heart Boy Mercy Dash Plane Crash Report Cover-up Denial', but I live in hope.

AEIOU

If you were asked to give a word containing the five vowels A, E, I, O, U, in that order, you might think of the word *facetious* or possibly of *abstemious*.

There are, of course, many other sequences in which these five vowels may be ordered. Any mathematician will tell you that five objects can be arranged in 120 different ways. So there are 120 different sequences of the five vowels – and to prove it, here they are:

AEIOU	AIEOU	AOEIU	AUEIO
AEIUO	AIEUO	AOEUI	AUEOI
AEOIU	AIOEU	AOIEU	AUIEO
AEOUI	AIOUE	AOIUE	AUIOE
AEUIO	AIUEO	AOUEI	AUOEI
AEUOI	AIUOE	AOUIE	AUOIE
EAIOU	EIAOU	EOAIU	EUAIO
EAIUO	EIAUO	EOAUI	EUAOI
EAOIU	EIOAU	EOIAU	EUIAO
EAOUI	EIOUA	EOIUA	EUIOA
EAUIO	EIUAO	EOUAI	EUOAI
EAUOI	EIUOA	EOUIA	EUOIA
IAEOU	IEAOU	IOAEU	IUAEO
IAEUO	IEAUO	IOAUE	IUAOE
IAOEU	IEOAU	IOEAU	IUEAO
IAOUE	IEOUA	IOEUA	IUEOA
IAUEO	IEUAO	IOUAE	IUOAE
IAUOE	IEUOA	IOUEA	IUOEA
OAEIU	OEAIU	OIAEU	OUAEI
OAEUI	OEAUI	OIAUE	OUAIE
OAIEU	OEIAU	OIEAU	OUEAI
OAIUE	OEIUA	OIEUA	OUEIA
OAUEI	OEUAI	OIUAE	OUIAE
OAUIE	OEUIA	OIUEA	OUIEA
UAEIO	UEAIO	UIAEO	UOAEI
UAEOI	UEAOI	UIAOE	UOAIE
UAIEO	UEIAO	UIEAO	UOEAI
UAIOE	UEIOA	UIEOA	UOEIA
UAOEI	UEOAI	UIOAE	UOIAE
UAOIE	UEOIA	UIOEA	UOIEA

Do you think it is possible to find a word containing the five vowels in each of the 120 possible sequences? Have a go and see how many you can find.

To start you off on your task, have a dialogue with your favourite ambidextrous housemaid when she's in a state of euphoria and not being unsociable.

Multiple Beheadings

The game of BEHEADINGS was described on page 73. An interesting solo variation is to try to find as many words as you can that are capable of multiple beheading.

For example:

> Spin – Pin – In
> About – Bout – Out
> Strap – Trap – Rap
> Gland – Land – And
> Amorally – Morally – Orally – Rally – Ally

How many words of this type can you discover? What is the longest chain of beheadings you can find?

Word Squares

For anyone fascinated by words, creating word squares is among the most absorbing of pencil-and-paper pastimes. The idea is simply to form a square of different words reading the same vertically and horizontally.

Word squares date back thousands of years. Socrates and Aristotle loved them, and the ancient Romans enjoyed them, too. When a Roman site at Cirencester in Gloucestershire was being excavated, this Latin word square was discovered on a piece of wall plaster:

> R O T A S
> O P E R A
> T E N E T
> A R E P O
> S A T O R

This word square is extra special: it is palindromic; you can read the five words backward or upward and it is still a perfect word square – the same words in another arrangement. Arepo is a proper name, but the other words are legitimate Latin and actually form a sentence which, when translated, means something like 'Arepo, the sower, controls the wheels with an effort'.

Devising word squares of your own with up to five-letter words is relatively easy.

One-letter word square:

I

Two-letter word square:

T O
O N

Three-letter word square:

T A N
A R E
N E T

Four-letter word square:

O P A L
P I N E
A N O N
L E N S

Five-letter word square:

B L I S S
L U N C H
I N T E R
S C E N E
S H R E W

Devising squares with six- and seven-letter words is much more difficult, though it can be done.

Six-letter word Square:

E S T A T E
S H A V E N
T A L E N T
A V E R S E
T E N S E R
E N T E R S

Eight-letter word square:

```
A G A R I C U S
G E N E R A N T
A N A C O N D A
R E C A N T E R
I R O N W O R T
C A N T O N A L
U N D E R A G E
S T A R T L E D
```

Darryl Francis and Dmitri Borgmann are the world's leading authorities on word squares. They say that about 900 squares of nine-letter words have been constructed. Here is one of them:

Nine-letter word square:

```
F R A T E R I E S
R E G I M E N A L
A G I T A T I V E
T I T A N I T E S
E M A N A T I S T
R E T I T R A T E
I N I T I A T O R
E A V E S T O N E
S L E S T E R E D
```

The ultimate achievement is a ten-letter word square. Darryl and Dmitri managed to construct one after hitting on the brilliant idea of using tautonyms – words, like *yoyo, cancan* and *beri-beri*, that consist of two identical halves. Even so, they had to use the same word more than once within the word square.

Ten-letter word square:

```
O R A N G U T A N G
R A N G A R A N G A
A N D O L A N D O L
N G O T A N G O T A
G A L A N G A L A N
U R A N G U T A N G
T A N G A T A N G A
A N D O L A N D O L
N G O T A N G O T A
G A L A N G A L A N
```

Definitions:

Orangutang: orangutan. A spelling given by *Funk and Wagnalls New Standard Dictionary* (1946).

Rangaranga: In the Caroline Islands, a name for parsley fern growing in the cracks of old walls. Taken from *The Caroline Islands* by Frederick Christian (1899).

Andolandol: A Chinese fly, a tincture of which is used as a blistering agent. Taken from *An Illustrated Encyclopedic Medical Dictionary* by Frank Foster (1888).

Ngotangota: Town on the western shore of Lake Nyasa, now spelled Kota Kota. Taken from *Longman's Gazetteer of the World* by George Chisholm (1902).

Galangalan: A mountain in Sorsogon Province, Luzon Island, Philippines. Taken from *A Pronouncing Gazetteer and Geographical Dictionary of the Philippine Islands* by the U.S. War Department (1902).

Urangutang: The orangutan again – spelling given in *Oxford English Dictionary* (1933).

Tangatanga: A name for the trinity of ancient Peruvian divinities – Pachama, Virakotcha and Mamakotcha. Taken from *The Reader's Handbook of Allusions, References, Plots and Stories* by E. Cobham Brewer (1880).

The world still awaits the first eleven-letter word square. However, if you are new to the game, I suggest you stick initially to the five- or six-letter variety.

Alphabeticar

One way to make a tedious journey less tiresome is to study the number plates on the cars that pass you or that you pass. In this game the aim is to form the alphabet from A to Z from the letters in the number plates that you see. DAL782X or A268COF will give you A, BKX222W or B190DCW will give you B, and so on. You can collect two or three letters at a time from one number plate, providing they appear on the number plate both alphabetically and consecutively – which means that YAB547T will give you A *and* B but AYB547T will not.

When you have completed the alphabet from A to Z, you can then go on to complete the alphabet in reverse order from Z to A.

PART THREE
WORD PLAY

Anagrams, Palindromes, Pangrams and Lipograms

Anagrams

When you have turned the word *Pepsi-Cola* into *episcopal*, or the word *cart-horse* into *orchestral* or *dishonest* into *hedonists*, you have created an anagram — an arrangement of the letters in a word or phrase to form another word or phrase. Anagrams are said to have originated in the fourth century BC with the Greek poet Lycophron, and they have been popular in every period of history since then.

Among the longest one-word anagrams are the following:

Containerised	—	Inconsiderate
Discriminator	—	Doctrinairism
Cephalometric	—	Petrochemical
Interrogatives	—	Tergiversation
Vicepresidents	—	Predictiveness
Interosculates	—	Sansculotterie

The largest group of mutual one-word anagrams is:

Arets – Aster – Astre – Earst – Rates – Reast – Resat – Stare – Strae – Tares – Tears – Teras

('Arets' is an obsolete word meaning 'assigns'; 'astre' means hearth or home; 'earst' means 'formerly'; 'strae' is a Scots word for straw; and 'teras' is a medical word meaning 'monstrosity'.)

Anagrams become more interesting, however, when they relate in some way to the original word or phrase. Here is a selection of my favourite anagrams which change a word into something spectacularly apt:

ALPHABETICALLY	I play all the ABC
ANIMOSITY	Is no amity
ASTRONOMER	Moon-starer
CONSIDERATE	Care is noted
CONVERSATION	Voices rant on
DESEGREGATION	Negroes get aid
DISCONSOLATE	Is not solaced
ENDEARMENT	Tender name

LUBRICATION	Act – rub oil in
MEASUREMENTS	Man uses meter
MISREPRESENTATION	Interpret one amiss
PARISHIONER	I hire parson
PITTANCE	A cent tip
PREDESTINATION	I pertain to ends
PRESBYTERIAN	Best in prayer
PUNISHMENT	Nine thumps
REVOLUTION	Love to ruin
SAINTLINESS	Least in sins
SCHOOLMASTER	The classroom
SEPARATION	One is apart
SOFTHEARTEDNESS	Often sheds tears
STAGHOUNDS	A hunt's dogs
SUGGESTION	It eggs us on
TEMPESTUOUS	Seems put out
TRAGEDIAN	Egad, I rant
TRIBULATIONS	Is but on trial
UNDIPLOMATIC	Mad, unpolitic
UNIFORMITY	I form unity
UPHOLSTERERS	Restore plush
WAITRESS	A stew, sir?

And here are a few more, where a phrase is the subject of the anagram:

THE ARISTOCRACY	A rich Tory caste
BATHING GIRLS	In slight garb
THE BOARDING HOUSE	This abode o' hunger
CIRCUMSTANTIAL EVIDENCE	Actual crime isn't evinced
THE COUNTRYSIDE	No city dust here
FOOL'S PARADISE	So ideal for sap
FRENCH REVOLUTION	Violence run forth
HMS PINAFORE	Name for ship
INTEGRAL CALCULUS	Calculating rules
THE IRISH NATION	Oh, that is in Erin
MIDWINTER WEATHER	Wind, rime, wet earth
THE MONA LISA	No hat, a smile
THE MORSE CODE	Here come dots
THE NUDIST COLONY	No untidy clothes
POLICE PROTECTION	Let cop cope in riot
A SENTENCE OF DEATH	Faces one at the end
SILVER AND GOLD	Grand old evils
SLOT MACHINES	Cash lost in 'em

| SUSPENDED ANIMATION | Supine man is not dead |
| WESTERN UNION | No wire unsent |

The names of the great and famous are, of course, prime targets for the anagrammatist:

CLINT EASTWOOD	Old West action
DANTE GABRIEL ROSETTI	Greatest idealist born
FLORENCE NIGHTINGALE	Flit on, cheering angel!
HENRY WADSWORTH LONGFELLOW	Won half the new world's glory
INDIRA GANDHI	Had Indian rig
MADAME CURIE	Radium came
MARGARET THATCHER	Great charm threat
ROALD AMUNDSEN	Laud'd Norseman
RONALD REAGAN	An oral danger
WILLIAM SHAKESPEARE	We all make his praise

It is possible to spend many happy hours taking a popular phrase or the name of a well-known person and shuffling the letters to see if you can produce an apt and amusing anagram. Try it also with the names of your friends and acquaintances.

Anagrams are truly Ars Magna – the great art.

Antigrams

An antigram is a special sort of anagram which has a meaning opposite to that of the word or phrase from which it is derived. Thus *real fun* is what you don't have at a *funeral* and *enormity* is not *more tiny*.

Here are a few of my favourite antigrams:

FILLED	Ill-fed
VIOLENCE	Nice love
INFECTION	Fine tonic
MISFORTUNE	It's more fun
MILITARISM	I limit arms
EVANGELISTS	Evil's agents
DISCRETION	Is no credit
ADVERSARIES	Are advisers
PROTECTIONISM	Nice to imports
OLD MAN WINTER	Warm, indolent
A PICTURE OF HEALTH	Oft pale, I ache, hurt
THE MAN WHO LAUGHS	He's glum, won't ha-ha

Palindromes

It is sometimes claimed that the first palindrome was created in the Garden of Eden, when Adam introduced himself to Eve with the words 'Madam, I'm Adam' (and Eve replied, simply, 'Eve'). In fact, the first palindrome was even earlier than this, when Adam said to his creator 'Name me Man'.

A palindrome is a word, like *did*, *noon*, *level*, *civic*, *kayak*, *tenet* or *repaper*, or a phrase or sentence, like 'Enid and Edna dine', that reads the same backwards as forwards.

The longest known palindromic word is *saippuakauppias*. It is a 15-letter Finnish word meaning 'soap-seller'. In the language of the Cree Indians is the 12-letter *kinnikkinnik* – the name of a tobacco substitute made from dried leaves and bark.

The longest palindromic word in everyday English is *redivider*, with nine letters. Also with nine letters are *Malayalam* (a language spoken in southern India) and *Rotavator* (a registered trademark that has found its way into the dictionary). *Detartrated*, with eleven letters, is a contrived scientific term that has not yet reached the dictionary.

It is not easy to create palindromic sentences, if it is a requirement that they make sense. The palindromist works with a greatly reduced vocabulary – you might see the word *red* in a palindrome, for example, but you are not likely to see *black*, *brown* or *blue*. Nevertheless, there are some extremely ingenious palindromic sentences. Here is a selection of my favourites:

Evil I did dwell; lewd did I live.

No lemons, no melon.

Pull up if I pull up.

Yawn a more Roman way.

Deer frisk, sir, freed.

'Tis Ivan, on a visit.

Was it a car or a cat I saw?

Now, Ned, I am a maiden won.

Ten animals I slam in a net.

Was it Eliot's toilet I saw?

Some men interpret nine memos.

A rod, not a bar: a baton, Dora.

Draw no dray a yard onward.

Sums are not set as a test on Erasmus.

Evil is a name of a foeman, as I live.

Goddesses so pay a possessed dog.

No mists reign at Tangier, St. Simon!

He lived as a devil, eh?

Marge lets Norah see Sharon's telegram.

A man, a plan, a canal – Panama.

Some palindromes are attributed to the famous. The composer Henry Purcell is said to have remarked:

Egad, a base tone denotes a bad age.

And of course there is this palindrome attributed to the emperor Napoleon in exile:

Able was I ere I saw Elba.

Billy Graham, the evangelist, might have said:

'Amen' I call if I fill a cinema.

When palindromes get longer, sense tends to disappear. These, however, are very creditable:

Doc, note I dissent. A fast never prevents fatness. I diet on cod.

Mirth, sir, a gay asset? No, don't essay a garish trim.

Are we not drawn onwards, we Jews, drawn onward to new era?

Desserts I desire not, so long no lost one rise distressed.

Too far away, no mere clay or royal ceremony, a war afoot.

Now saw ye no mosses or foam, or aroma of roses. So money was won.

What must surely be the best long palindrome ever penned was the work of Joyce Johnson, and was written as an entry for a competition in the *New Statesman* in 1967. Here it is, all 467 letters of it:

HEADMASTER'S PALINDROMIC LIST ON HIS MEMO PAD

Test on Erasmus

Deliver slap

Royal: phone no.?

Ref. Football.

Is sofa sitable on?

XI – staff over

Sub-edit Nurse's order

Caning is on test (snub slip-up)

Birch (Sid) to help Miss Eve

Repaper den

Use it

Put inkspot on stopper

Prof. – no space

Caretaker (wall, etc.)

Too many d— pots

Wal for duo? (I'd name Dr O)

See few owe fees (or demand IOU?)

Dr of Law

Stop dynamo (OTC)

Tel: Law re Kate Race

Caps on for prep

Pots – no tops

Knit up ties ('U')

Ned (re paper)

Eve's simple hot dish (crib)

Pupil's buns

T-set: no sign in a/c

Red roses

Run Tide Bus?

Rev off at six

Noel Bat is a fossil

Lab to offer one 'Noh' play

– or 'Pals Reviled'?

Sums are not set.

Pseudodromes

Pseudodromes are palindromes in which words, rather than individual letters, read the same backwards or forwards. Pseudodromes may not be true palindromes but they can be quite as entertaining, as these examples demonstrate:

So patient a doctor to doctor a patient so.

Does milk machinery milk does?

Bores are people that say that people are bores.

Women understand men; few men understand women.

Dollars make men covetous, then covetous men make dollars.

You can cage a swallow, can't you, but you can't swallow a cage, can you?

Girl, bathing on Bikini, eyeing boy, finds boy eyeing bikini on bathing girl.

Pangrams

The quick brown fox jumps over a lazy dog.

That well-known sentence, often used as a typing test, is an example of a pangram — a sentence that uses every letter of the alphabet. That particular pangram uses 33 letters, but there are shorter pangrams:

Pack my box with five dozen liquor jugs.	(32 letters)
Quick waxy bugs jump the frozen veldt.	(31 letters)
The five boxing wizards jump quickly.	(31 letters)
Jackdaws love my big sphinx of quartz.	(31 letters)
How quickly daft jumping zebras vex.	(30 letters)

To get below 30 letters, you have to introduce proper names:

Quick wafting zephyrs vex bold Jim.	(29 letters)
Waltz, nymph, for quick jigs vex Bud.	(28 letters)

The ultimate, of course, is a pangram consisting of only 26 letters. These are examples, but they use either initials and funny names or obscure archaic and dialect words:

Blowzy night-frumps vex'd Jack Q.

J. Q. Schwartz flung D. V. Pike my box.

Cwm fjord-bank glyphs vext quiz.

This latter may be translated as 'Ancient inscriptions on the side of a fjord in a Welsh valley annoyed an eccentric'.

If you can devise the perfect 26-letter pangram, it may not make you rich but it will certainly make you famous.

If you can't devise pangrams of your own, you can look for them in pieces of literature. When reading the Book of Ezra, Chapter 7, Verse 21, you will have been struck by the following sentence:

And I, even I Ataxerxes the king, do make a decree to all the treasurers which are beyond the river, that whatsoever Ezra the priest, the scribe of the law of the God of heaven, shall require of you, it be done speedily.

That is an imperfect pangram because it lacks the letter J. Also imperfect as a pangram, lacking the letter Z, are these lines from Shakespeare's *Coriolanus*:

> O! a kiss
> Long as my exile, sweet as my revenge!
> Now, by the jealous queen of heaven, that kiss
> I carried from thee, dear, and my true lip
> Hath virgin'd it ever since.

A true pangram, however, may be found in the following lines from Milton's *Paradise Lost*:

> Likening his Maker to the grazed ox,
> Jehovah, who, in one night, when he passed
> From Egypt marching, equalled with one stroke
> Both her first-born and all her bleating gods.

There must be many more pangrams waiting to be found in works of great literature, so get those neglected classics down from the shelf and start searching. Then you might be able to say:

By Jove, my quick study of lexicography won a prize.

Lipograms

A lipogram is a literary text in which one or more letters of the alphabet have been deliberately excluded.

Among the great lipograms of the past were the poet Tryphiodorus who wrote an epic poem about the adventures of Ulysses, omitting a different letter of the Greek alphabet from each of its 24 books; and Lope de Vega, the prolific Spanish dramatist, who wrote five novels excluding the letters A, E, I, O and U in turn.

Coming to the present century, the 50,000 word novel *Gadsby* by Ernest Vincent Wright, published in 1939, was written completely without the use of the letter E.

There is not enough space to reproduce any of these works here. But we can show some of the work of the contemporary lipogrammarian A. Ross Eckler, who rewrote the nursery rhyme *Mary Had A Little Lamb* in several versions, omitting various common letters.

Here, to remind you, is the original verse:

Mary had a little lamb,
Its fleece was white as snow,
And everywhere that Mary went
The lamb was sure to go;
It followed her to school one day,
That was against the rule;
It made the children laugh and play
To see a lamb in school.

Now here are three of Mr Eckler's versions, omitting the letters H, T and E in turn:

Mary owned a little lamb,
Its fleece was pale as snow,
And every place its mistress went
It certainly would go;
It followed Mary to class one day,
It broke a rigid law;
It made some students giggle aloud,
A lamb in class all saw.

Mary had a pygmy lamb,
His fleece was pale as snow,
And every place where Mary walked
Her lamb did also go;
Her lamb came inside her classroom once,
Which broke a rigid rule;
How children all did laugh and play
On seeing a lamb in school.

Mary had a tiny lamb,
Its wool was pallid as snow,
And any spot that Mary did walk
This lamb would always go;
This lamb did follow Mary to school,
Although against a law;
How girls and boys did laugh and play,
That lamb in class all saw.

Composing lipograms, as well as being great fun, is a valuable exercise in that it teaches one to express the same idea in different ways. Why not see if you can do as well with other works? Try producing alternative versions of other nursery rhymes or short poems, omitting some common letter. Then perhaps you might care to tackle the works of

Shakespeare. I myself have had a go at *Hamlet*, from which I scrupulously excluded the letter I. Here is part of it:

> To be, or not to be; that's the query:
> Whether you would be nobler to suffer mentally
> The stones and arrows of outrageous fortune,
> Or to take arms to oppose a sea of troubles,
> And through combat end them? To pass on, to sleep:
> No more . . .

I cannot leave the subject of the lipogram without including the following example which, I am sure, must be unique. This work, by an unknown author, is a pangrammatic lipogram – or is it a lipogrammatic pangram? Each stanza of this poem has been written so that it includes all the letters of the alphabet except E.

THE FATE OF NASSAN

> Bold Nassan quits his caravan,
> A hazy mountain grot to scan;
> Climbs craggy rocks to spy his way,
> Doth tax his sight, but far doth stray.
>
> Not work of man, nor sport of child,
> Finds Nassan in that mazy wild;
> Lax grow his joints, limbs toil in vain –
> Poor wight! why didst thou quit that plain?
>
> Vainly for succour Nassan calls,
> Know, Zillah, that thy Nassan falls;
> But prowling wolf and fox may joy,
> To quarry on thy Arab boy.

Clangers

Spoonerisms

A spoonerism is the transposition (either accidentally or deliberately) of the initial letters of the words in a phrase so as to change the phrase's meaning or make nonsense of it.

A well-boiled icicle.

The Lord is a shoving leopard.

Please sew me to another sheet.

Let us toast the queer old dean.

I have in my bosom a half-warmed fish.

You were fighting a liar in the quadrangle.

The cat popped on its drawers.

You have hissed my mystery lectures; you have tasted a whole worm. You will leave Oxford by the town drain.

These classic spoonerisms have all been attributed to the Reverend William Spooner, Warden of New College, Oxford from 1903 to 1924, but it is doubtful if any of them ever issued from his lips. Despite being a shrewd man of considerable personal dignity, he was apparently what most people would consider 'an absent-minded professor'. He did, it seems, give out a hymn in chapel as *Kinquering Kongs Their Titles Take*, and he did use the words 'In a dark, glassly'. On meeting Stanley Casson in the quadrangle, Dr Spooner said to him 'Do come to dinner tonight to meet Casson, our new Fellow.' 'But, Warden, I *am* Casson,' said Casson, to which Spooner replied 'Never mind, come all the same.'

Spooner, however, vigorously denied authorship of the classic spoonerisms attributed to him, and it is almost certain that they are the invention of Oxford undergraduates who, inspired by the verbal infelicities of the Doctor, enthusiastically took up the idea of creating spoonerisms by design rather than accident.

Why not have a go at inventing some spoonerisms of your own? I can assure you the exercise will provide plots of leisure.

Malapropisms

A malapropism, named after the character Mrs Malaprop in Sheridan's play *The Rivals*, is a ludicrous misuse of words, especially by confusion with similar words. Here are a few highlights from the conversation of Mrs Malaprop herself:

'A progeny of learning.'

'Make no delusions to the past.'

'She's as headstrong as an allegory on the banks of the Nile.'

'Illiterate him, I say, quite from your memory.'

'An aspersion upon my parts of speech! Was ever such a brute! Sure, if I reprehend anything in this world, it is the use of my oracular tongue, and a nice derangement of epitaphs!'

Here are a few of my favourites among the more modern malapropisms I have heard or read:

'White as the dripping snow.'

'I was so surprised you could have knocked me over with a fender.'

'I was so hungry that I gouged myself.'

'My sister uses massacre on her eyes.'

'He had to use biceps to deliver the baby.'

'I don't like him and he doesn't like me, so it's neutral.'

'I had an idea that would happen – I must be psychopathic.'

If you want to form your own collection of malapropisms, I can recommend disc jockeys and sports commentators on TV or radio as a good source of erogenous phraseology.

Goldwynisms

Sam Goldwyn, the Hollywood movie mogul, was renowned for his verbal clangers. It is impossible to define the essence of a Goldwynism – each one is unique. All one can do is regard them with awestruck admiration.

'Include me out.'

'In two words: im-possible!'

'A verbal contract isn't worth the paper it's written on.'

'We're overpaying him, but he's worth it.'

'We have all passed a lot of water since then.'

'I'll give you a definite maybe.'

'If Roosevelt were alive, he'd turn over in his grave.'

'It's more than magnificent – it's mediocre.'

'Anybody who goes to see a psychiatrist ought to have his head examined.'

'Every director bites the hand that lays the golden egg.'

'Yes, my wife's hands are very beautiful. I'm going to have a bust made of them.'

'I read part of it all the way through.'

'Let's have some new clichés.'

'A bachelor's life is no life for a single man.'

'Going to call him William? What kind of a name is that? Every Tom, Dick and Harry's called William. Why don't you call him Bill?'

Mixed Metaphors

We all mix metaphors all the time. Even Shakespeare was susceptible. In Hamlet's great soliloquy the words 'to take arms against a sea of trouble' are a classic example of a mixed metaphor.

Mixed metaphors are part of everyday speech and usually we don't even notice. 'To hog the limelight', 'galloping inflation', 'a fully-fledged star', 'to latch on to a new hobby' are examples. It is only when the metaphors that are mixed present a startlingly incongruous image in our minds that the mixed metaphor becomes worthy of our notice. Like these gems:

He is a rough diamond with a heart of gold.

It is the thin end of a white elephant.

The sacred cows have come home to roost with a vengeance.

All these white sepulchres are tarred with the same brush.

The views of the grass roots are not hearing the light of day.

Wild horses on their bended knees would not make me do it.

The whole chain of events consists entirely of missing links.

I strongly protest against the attack on my absent friend, for surely it is not right to hang a man behind his back.

One of the most famous of all mixed metaphors comes from a speech made in the House of Commons by the eighteenth-century Irish politician Sir Boyle Roche:

Mr. Speaker, I smell a rat: I see him forming in the air and darkening the sky: but I'll nip him in the bud.

Poetry And Rhyme

Limericks

> The limerick is furtive and mean;
> You must keep her in close quarantine,
>   Or she sneaks to the slums
>   And promptly becomes
> Disorderly, drunk and obscene.

A limerick is a five-line nonsense verse that originated with the eighteenth-century ale-house chorus 'Will you come up to Limerick' and was later made famous by Edward Lear.

> Although at the limericks of Lear
> We may be tempted to sneer
>   We should never forget
>   That we owe him a debt
> For his work as the first pioneer.

It must be said that the majority of limericks are lewd and indecent. There are some, though, that are amusing without being offensive. Here is a very brief selection of my favourites:

> There was an old fellow of Tring
> Who, when someone asked him to sing,
>   Replied 'Ain't it odd?
>   I can never tell *God*
> *Save The Weasel* from *Pop Goes The King*.

> There was a young fellow of Perth
> Who was born on the day of his birth;
>   He married, they say,
>   On his wife's wedding day,
> And he died when he quitted the earth.

> There was an old man of Madrid
> Who ate sixty eggs — yes, he did!
>   When they asked 'Are you faint?'
>   He replied 'No, I ain't.
> But I don't feel as well as I did.'

I sat next to the Duchess at tea;
It was just as I feared it would be.
  Her rumblings abdominal
  Were simply phenomenal,
And everyone thought it was me!

There was a faith-healer of Deal
Who said 'Although pain isn't real,
  If I sit on a pin
  And it punctures my skin,
I dislike what I fancy I feel.'

Some of my favourite limericks take liberties with spelling:

Said a maid 'I will marry for lucre'
And her scandalized ma almost shucre.
  But when the chance came
  And she told the good dame,
I notice she did not rebucre.

There was a young lady named Wemyss
Who, it semyss, was afflicted with dremyss.
  She would wake in the night
  And in terrible fright
Shake the bemyss of the house with her scremyss.

Writing limericks of your own can provide a great deal of fun, and it is not too difficult to produce an acceptable result – that is, if you avoid the error made by the young man from Japan:

There was a young man from Japan
Whose limericks never would scan.
  When asked why that was,
  He replied 'It's because
I always try to cram as many words into the last line
  as I possibly can.'

Clerihews

Edmund Clerihew Bentley is remembered mainly for his classic detective story *Trent's Last Case* and for the verse form that was named after him – the clerihew.

Bentley's first collection of verse in this vein was published in 1905 as *Biography For Beginners*. Further collections appeared in 1929 and in 1939. It was soon after the publication of the first volume that the name 'clerihew' became applied to this particular form of light verse.

What exactly is a clerihew? Frances Stillman in *The Poet's Manual and Rhyming Dictionary* defines it as 'a humorous pseudo-biographical quatrain, rhymed as two couplets, with lines of uneven length more or less in the rhythm of prose'. Add to this, that the name of the subject usually ends the first or, less often, the second line, and that the humour of the clerihew is whimsical rather than satiric, and that it is a verse form comparatively unknown outside the UK, and there you have a complete definition.

Here are a few of my favourite Bentley clerihews:

> The people of Spain think Cervantes
> Equal to half-a-dozen Dantes;
> An opinion resented most bitterly
> By the people of Italy.

> Although Machiavelli
> Was extremely fond of jelly,
> He stuck religiously to mince
> While he was writing *The Prince*.

> George the Third
> Ought never to have occurred.
> One can only wonder
> At so grotesque a blunder.

> Among the contemporaries of Shakespeare
> There were few who regarded him as Drake's peer.
> Spoiling paper was so much less strain
> Than spoiling the Spanish Main.

> Sir Humphrey Davy
> Abominated gravy.
> He lived in the odium
> Of having discovered sodium.

And here are three clerihews by Michael Curl:

> Alexander Selkirk
> Did not like hotel work.
> He informed a maid
> That he was monarch of all he surveyed.

James Joyce
Had an extremely loud voice;
In the morning he'd shout and make
Finnegans Wake.

E. C. Bentley
Mused while he ought to have studied intently;
It was this muse
That inspired clerihews.

Sententious Verse

The object of the game is to write the longest piece of verse that you can, consisting of *only one sentence*. To give you something to aim for, here is a forty-eight-line example by John Slim:

DEATH SENTENCE

Have you heard how Cuthbert Hatch
To find a gas leak, struck a match
And thereby hastened his despatch
To realms unknown to you and me,
Who have not yet been foolishly
Inclined to leave posterity
To puzzle for itself just why
We chose to make our fragments fly
For ever upwards to the sky,
As Cuthbert did when in the dark
He smelled a smell and sparked a spark
Which sent him rising like a lark
– A very shattered fowl, it's true,
With no lump large enough to stew
And nothing any cat could chew –
Into the unresisting space
Where there is never any place
To rest one's feet or wash one's face,
Though this, for faceless, feetless folk,
As Cuthbert was by then, poor bloke,
Is not by any means a yoke
Which is impossible to bear,
For it's with truth that I declare
That cases are extremely rare

Of people ceasing to exist
And then, assuming they'll be missed,
Proceeding forthwith to insist
On spreading sadness with their pen
Among their former fellow-men
With news of things beyond their ken
By writing letters to the Press
To say that they are in a mess
Which words in print cannot express,
For they're aware that we below
Quite rarely care just how they go
And, once they've gone, don't want to know
The finer details of the fate
Which suddenly transformed their state
From Man Alive into The Late
Lamented such as Cuthbert Hatch,
Who found that leak with lighted match
And who thereafter failed to catch
The interest of the public eye
Or stir mankind to spare a sigh
– Which may explain precisely why
I think that Cuthbert Hatch (The Late)
Would not expect to read (or rate)
A second sentence on his fate?

By Apt Alliteration's Artful Aid

We are all familiar with alliteration as one of the weapons in the poet's armoury. Few poets, however, used alliteration to the same extent as the writer of that epic ballad *The Siege Of Belgrade* – that great poet Anon.

THE SIEGE OF BELGRADE

An Austrian army, awfully arrayed,
Boldly, by battery, besieged Belgrade;
Cossack commanders cannonading come –
Dealing destruction's devastating doom;
Every endeavour, engineers essay,
For fame, for fortune – fighting furious fray: –
Generals 'gainst generals grapple – gracious God!
How honours heaven, heroic hardihood!
Infuriate – indiscriminate in ill,

Kindred kill kinsmen, – kinsmen kindred kill!
Labour low levels loftiest, longest lines –
Men march 'mid mounds, 'mid moles, 'mid murderous mines:
Now noisy, noxious, noticed nought
Of outward obstacles opposing ought;
Poor patriots, partly purchased, partly pressed;
Quite quaking, quickly quarter, quarter quest,
Reason returns, religious right redounds,
Sorrow stops such sanguinary sounds.
Truce to thee, Turkey – triumph to thy train!
Unjust, unwise, unmerciful Ukraine!
Vanish vain victory, vanish victory vain!
Why wish ye warfare? Wherefore welcome were
Xerxes, Ximenes, Xanthus, Xaviere?
Yield! ye youths! ye yeomen, Yield, your yell!
Zeono's, Zapater's, Zoroaster's zeal,
And all attracting – arms against acts appeal.

As an example of alphabetical alliteration this is not quite perfect –
note that the author skipped *j* and there is a *ye* in among the *w*'s. But
could you do any better?

Acrostics

An acrostic is a verse in which a word or a message or (most commonly) a
name is spelled out by the initial letters of the lines.

Lewis Carroll loved to create acrostics, and here is his most famous
example, dedicated to Alice Pleasance Liddell, the little girl who
inspired *Alice's Adventures in Wonderland*:

A boat, beneath a sunny sky
Lingering onward dreamily
In an evening of July –

Children three that nestle near,
Eager eye and willing ear,
Pleased a simple tale to hear –

Long has paled that sunny sky;
Echoes fade and memories die:
Autumn frosts have slain July.

Still she haunts me, phantomwise,
Alice moving under skies
Never seen by waking eyes.

Children yet the tale to hear,
Eager eye and willing ear,
Lovingly shall nestle near.

In Wonderland they lie,
Dreaming as the days go by,
Dreaming as the summers die:

Ever drifting down the stream –
Lingering in the golden gleam –
Life, what is it but a dream?

Single-Rhymed Verse

An interesting exercise is to see what is the longest piece of verse one can produce using only a single rhyme. Clearly you have to pick your rhyme carefully – you would get further if you ended your first line with the word *man*, for example, than you would if it ended with *rhythm* or *silver*!

Here, to show you what can be achieved, is a single-rhyme alphabet dating from the nineteenth century.

A was an Army, to settle disputes;
B was a Bull, not the mildest of brutes;
C was a Cheque, duly drawn upon Coutts;
D was King David, with harps and with lutes;
E was an Emperor, hailed with salutes;
F was a Funeral, followed by mutes;
G was a Gallant in Wellington boots;
H was a Hermit who lived upon roots;
I was Justinian his Institutes;
K was a Keeper, who commonly shoots;
L was a Lemon, the sourest of fruits;
M was a Ministry – say Lord Bute's;
N was Nicholson, famous on flutes;
O was an Owl, that hisses and hoots;
P was a Pond, full of leeches and newts;
Q was a Quaker, in whitey-brown suits;

R was a Reason, which Paley refutes;
S was a Sergeant with twenty recruits;
T was Ten Tories of doubtful reputes;
U was Uncommonly bad cheroots;
V Vicious motives, Which malice imputes;
X an Ex-King driven out by emeutes;
Y is a Yarn; then, the last rhyme that suits,
Z is the Zuyder Zee, dwelt in by coots.

Univocalics

Univocalic verse restricts itself to the use of only one vowel. Here is a well-known, though brief example, of the art:

> Persevere, ye perfect men,
> Ever keep the precepts ten.

And here is a Victorian production, on the theme of the Russo-Turkish war, using A as the only vowel:

> War harms all ranks, all arts, all crafts appal;
> At Mars' harsh blast, arch, rampart, altar fall!
> Ah! hard as adamant a braggart Czar
> Arms vassal-swarms, and fans a fatal war!
> Rampant at that bad call, a Vandal band
> Harass, and harm, and ransack Wallach-land.
> A Tartar phalanx Balkan's scarp hath past,
> And Allah's standard falls, alas! at last.

Puns And Riddles

Puns

The glorious paradox of the pun is that the worse it is the better it is.
When you have heard a pleasing pun you don't show your appreciation
by laughing – you groan instead. Puns are plays on words using the same
or similar sounds, and they come in all shapes and sizes.

There are short, snappy ones:

> A yes-man is one who stoops to concur.

> When I'm stoned I get a little boulder.

> Corporal punishment smacks of sadism.

There are long rambling puns:

> Little Jimmy was looking forward to going to the circus with his
> Uncle Alf. When the day arrived, his father said 'I'm afraid Uncle
> Alf can't take you to the circus today. He's gone to Wimbledon to
> watch the tennis instead.' 'But I didn't even know Uncle Alf liked
> tennis' wailed little Jimmy. 'Oh yes,' said his father, 'I've often
> heard Alfred laud tennis, son.'

> A newspaper editor was dining in a very grand French restaurant
> in Mayfair, and he enthused about the Coq au Vin. Summoning
> the proprietor of the restaurant, he asked if he could have the
> recipe. 'Oh no,' replied the proprietor. 'In the restaurant business
> we are just like you journalists – we never reveal our sauces.'

There are heavenly puns:

> Saint Peter: And how did you get here?
> Latest arrival: Flu.

And hellish puns:

> Latest arrival: Do you mind if I smoke?
> Little devil: I don't mind if you burn.

There are alcoholic puns:

> 'Orange juice sorry you made me cry?'
> 'Don't be soda pressed – them martini bruises.'

And there are philosophical puns:

> Better to have loved a short girl
> Than never to have loved a tall.

Few great writers have resisted altogether the temptation to indulge in the occasional pun and some, like Shakespeare, revelled in it. In that play, Lady Macbeth says:

> 'If he do bleed
> I'll gild the faces of the grooms withal;
> For it must seem their guilt.'

If punning is not to your taste, don't worry. It's well known that one man's Mede is another man's Persian.

Tom Swifties

Named after a character in a series of books by Edward Statemeyer, published in the 1920s, Tom Swifties are a type of pun for which there seems to be a craze every few years. The idea is to make a pun on an adverb or adverbial phrase, as in the following examples:

> 'Let's trap that sick bird,' said Tom illegally.

> 'Pass the cards,' said Tom ideally.

> 'I like to go camping,' said Tom intently.

> 'That's a very large herring,' said Tom superficially.

> 'I've just had a serious operation,' said Tom half-heartedly.

> 'Drop that gun!' said Tom disarmingly.

> 'The bacon is burnt,' said Tom with panache.

> 'Turn on the radio,' said Tom with a short wave.

> 'How about a game of draughts?' asked Tom airily.

'Try looking in the attic,' said Tom loftily.

'I've swallowed a lot of hay,' said Tom balefully.

Croakers

The croaker is a close relative of Tom Swiftie, and in this case the pun is purely verbal, as these examples demonstrate:

'I'm dying,' he croaked.

'The fire is going out,' he bellowed.

'Someone is at the door,' she chimed.

'I ordered raspberry ripple not vanilla,' I screamed.

'Watch the birdie!' he snapped.

'We've struck oil,' he gushed.

'I think company's coming,' she guessed.

Terse Verse

The world's greatest punster is Alan F. G. Lewis, who has made creating puns his life's work. Many of his puns are cast in a form he calls Terse Verse. Here are some of my favourites:

Soupçon is French for a small amount, only morceau.

Schnapps and hock are my favourite Teutonics.

If his new secretary isn't sweet in the daytime and a little tart at night, he'll saccharin the morning.

Why piccolo profession like music that's full of viol practices, confirmed lyres, old fiddles, and bass desires?
For the lute, of course.

I'll be with you –
in two sex, said the hermaphrodite
in half a tick, said the vivisectionist

in two shakes, said the freemason
in half a mho, said the electrician
in a trice, said the Third Man
in necks to no time, said the executioner
in a flash, said the magician
in an instant, said the marketing man
in a twinkling, eye said.

I Told Her

I told her no sensible man
would take her dancing
in her bikini.
So she went
with a little moron.

Valentine Rhyme

My heart and I
Call to you
But you're too deaf
To Eros.

The Tree of Love

Yew witch Hazel
It's plane
I'm sycamore poplar girls
And aspen alder time
On the beech
And pine to cedar day
When I maple to say
'Hazel lime yours,
Cumquat may.'

Please Be Seated

When she said 'Howdah do
Take a pew
You look divan'
I thought 'This is sit'
But I was throne aside
When she decided to settle
For a pouffe.

A sort of plinth charming
Who promised to support her
For the rest of her dais,
Next time I'll be more chairy.

The Poet's Dilemma

Once upon a time I used
To mispel
To sometimes split infinitives
To get words of out order
To punctuate, – badly
To confused my tenses
To deem old words wondrous fair
to ignore capitals
To employ common or garden clichés
To miss the occasional out
To indulge in tautological repetitive statements
To exaggerate hundreds of times a day
And to repeat puns quite by chants
But worst of all I used
To forget to finish what I

Not The Nine O'Clock News

The clichés used in news reports on radio and television often provide material for the inveterate punster:

Hundreds of stray dogs disappeared yesterday. Police say they have no leads.

A truck carrying strawberries spilled its load at a busy intersection today. The result was a large traffic jam.

Two men robbed a city bank today. One of the men is described as being seven feet tall, and the other is said to be four feet six inches. The police are looking high and low for them.

After a Japanese motor factory was hit by a tornado earlier this week, witnesses say it has been raining Datsun cogs.

A lorry carrying onions has shed its load on the motorway. Motorists are advised to find a hard shoulder to cry on.

Thieves stole a van containing bottles of hair restorer, but their getaway ended when it crashed over a bridge. Police are now combing the area.

Dismissals

When a man loses his job he may be dismissed, sacked, fired or kicked out; he may be out on his ear or on his neck; he may be shown the door; or he may be given his cards, his marching orders, the push, the elbow, the old heave-ho or the order of the boot.

Some professions, however, have their own individual terminology for this situation: a clergyman is defrocked, a lawyer disbarred, an army officer cashiered.

Why should not people in other walks of life also have their own terms for dismissal? Thus:

> An office-worker could be defiled.
> A salesman could be disordered.
> A writer could be described.
> A journalist could be depressed.
> A wine merchant could be deported.
> A celebrity could be defamed.
> A climber could be dismounted.
> A jailer could be excelled.
> A policeman could be unwarranted.
> A judge could be dishonoured.
> A bishop could be disgraced.
> A model could be deposed.
> A prostitute could be delayed.
> A Moonie could be dissected.
> A conjuror could be disillusioned.
> A rabble-rouser could be demobbed.
> A musician could be denoted, disbarred, disbanded,
>   decomposed or disconcerted!

See how many more 'dismissals' you can think of.

Awful Authors

This is a form of word play, especially popular among children, which involves inventing the name of an imaginary author punningly alluding to the name of an equally imaginary book.

The most satisfactory results are obtained when the names of the authors are reasonably credible while at the same time containing the most outrageous puns.

Here are some of my favourites, but no doubt you can come up with better examples:

Dog's Dinner by Nora Bone
The Gardener by Moses Lawn
Slimming by Lena Boddy
The Open Window by Eileen Doubt
The Debtor by Owen Munny
Crime Does Pay by Robin Banks
The Funeral by Paul Bearer
The Female Ghost by Sheila Peer
The Lion Tamer by Claude Face
Frankenstein Meets Dracula by Horace Tory
King Kong by Hugh Jape
The Singer by Barry Tone
Big White Bird by Albert Ross
A Visit To The Dentist by Phil McAvity
The Cavalryman by Rhoda Norse
A Continental Breakfast by Roland Coffy
Where's My Hat by Sonia Head
Prehistoric Reptiles by Terry Dactyl & Dinah Soar
Tolstoi by Warren Peace
D-Day by Norman D. Landing
At The Eleventh Hour by Justin Time

Riddles

Riddles are the most ancient and most widespread type of word game. They have been popular in every civilization and every culture, both ancient and modern.

Having said that, it must be admitted that the traditional riddle is not quite the same as the wordplay we know by that name today. The traditional riddle is a cryptic or enigmatic utterance which the hearer has to try to interpret. An example is in the Story of Samson who, having seen a swarm of bees making honey in the carcass of a lion, proposed the riddle:

> Out of the eater came something to eat;
> Out of the strong came something sweet.

By contrast, the modern riddle is usually based on a pun, and the aim is amusement rather than mystification.

There are riddles based on letters of the alphabet:

Q. Which letter is like a Roman emperor?
A. P – because it is near O.

Q. Which other letters are like a Roman emperor?
A. The C's are.

Q. Why is the letter D like a naughty child?
A. Because it makes ma mad.

One popular form may be styled the 'Difference' riddle:

Q. What's the difference between a poor man and a feather bed?
A. One is hard up, the other is soft down.

Q. What's the difference between a woman and a postage stamp?
A. One is a female, the other a mail fee.

Q. What's the difference between an ornithologist and someone who can't spell?
A. One is a bird-watcher, the other is a word-botcher.

Q. What's the difference between a cat and a comma?
A. A cat has claws at the end of its paws, a comma is a pause at the end of a clause.

Another popular type is the 'Crossing' riddle:

Q. What do you get if you cross an elephant with a kangaroo?
A. Great big holes all over Australia.

Q. What do you get if you cross a hyena with a stallion?
A. Hoarse laughter.

Q. What do you get if you cross a weasel with a nightingale?
A. A pop singer.

In fact there is a wide variety of riddles, covering just about every subject one can think of.

Q. Where do sheep go to have their hair cut?
A. The baa-baa shop.

Q. What lies on the sea-bed and trembles?
A. A nervous wreck.

Q. What's a Grecian urn?
A. About ten drachmas a week.

Q. How do you use an Egyptian doorbell?
A. Toot-and-come-in.

Q. Why do devils and ghosts get on well together?
A. Because demons are a ghouls best friends.

Q. Why were the Dark Ages dark?
A. Because there were so many knights.

Q. Do any metals float on water?
A. Tin can but stainless steel sinks.

Q. Why does a calendar have only a year to live?
A. Because its days are numbered.

Q. What flies the Atlantic and climbs the Empire State Building?
A. King Kongcorde.

Q. What colours are the sun and wind?
A. The sun rose and the wind blue.

ALPHABETICAL LIST OF GAMES